First World War
and Army of Occupation
War Diary
France, Belgium and Germany

40 DIVISION
121 Infantry Brigade
Suffolk Regiment
12th Battalion
27 May 1916 - 31 May 1918

WO95/2616/1

The Naval & Military Press Ltd
www.nmarchive.com
Published in association with The National Archives

Published by

The Naval & Military Press Ltd

Unit 10 Ridgewood Industrial Park,

Uckfield, East Sussex,

TN22 5QE England

Tel: +44 (0) 1825 749494

www.naval-military-press.com

www.nmarchive.com

This diary has been reprinted in facsimile from the original. Any imperfections are inevitably reproduced and the quality may fall short of modern type and cartographic standards.

© Crown Copyright
Images reproduced by permission of The National Archives, London, England, 2015.

Contents

Document type	Place/Title	Date From	Date To
Heading	WO95/2616/1		
Heading	40th Division 121st Infy Bde 12th Bn Suffolk Regt Jun 1916-May 1918 From UK To 14 Div 43 Bde		
War Diary	Pirbright	27/05/1916	04/06/1916
War Diary	Southampton	05/06/1916	05/06/1916
War Diary	Le Havre	06/06/1916	06/06/1916
War Diary	Lillers	07/06/1916	09/06/1916
War Diary	Chocques	09/06/1916	09/06/1916
War Diary	Labeuvriere	09/06/1916	12/06/1916
War Diary	Liliers	17/06/1916	19/06/1916
War Diary	Barlin	21/06/1916	24/06/1916
War Diary	Calonne	24/06/1916	28/06/1916
Heading	War Diary. of 12th (S) Battalion Suffolk Regiment. from 1st July, 1916 to 31st July, 1916		
War Diary	Barlin	01/07/1916	02/07/1916
War Diary	Maroc	03/07/1916	11/07/1916
War Diary	Les Brebis	12/07/1916	16/07/1916
War Diary	Maroc	17/07/1916	22/07/1916
War Diary	Loos	22/07/1916	31/07/1916
Heading	War Diary of 1st (S) Bn Suffolk Regt. from aug 1st 1916 to aug 31st 1916 Volume. 3.		
War Diary	Loos	01/08/1916	04/08/1916
War Diary	N. Maroc	05/08/1916	09/08/1916
War Diary	Les Brebis	10/08/1916	12/08/1916
War Diary	S Maroc	13/08/1916	19/08/1916
War Diary	N. Maroc	21/08/1916	31/08/1916
Heading	War Diary of 12th Bn Suffolk Regt From Sept 1st 1916 To Sept. 30th 1916 Volume IV		
War Diary	S. Maroc	01/09/1916	05/09/1916
War Diary	Les Brebis	06/09/1916	19/09/1916
War Diary	Loos	11/09/1916	22/09/1916
War Diary	N Maroc	23/09/1916	26/09/1916
War Diary	Loos	27/09/1916	30/09/1916
Heading	War Diary of 12th Bn Suffolk Regt. From Oct 1st 1916 To Oct 31st 1916 Vol 5		
Miscellaneous	Perforated Sheet giving detail of personnel and horses wanting to complete, shown on Army From B. 213		
Miscellaneous	Field Return.		
Miscellaneous	Officers and men who have become casuals, been transferred or joined since last report.		
War Diary	Loos	01/10/1916	08/10/1916
War Diary	N. Maroc	09/10/1916	12/10/1916
War Diary	Mazingarbe	13/10/1916	13/10/1916
War Diary	14 Bis	14/10/1916	22/10/1916
War Diary	Mazingarbe	23/10/1916	27/10/1916
War Diary	Les Brebis	28/10/1916	28/10/1916
War Diary	Bruay	29/10/1916	29/10/1916
War Diary	Chelers	30/10/1916	31/10/1916
Heading	War Diary of 12th (S) Bn Suffolk Regt. From 1/11/16 To 30/11/16 Volume VI		

Miscellaneous			
Miscellaneous	For information of the A.G.'s Office at the Base. Officers and men who have become casuals, been transferred or joined since last report.		
Miscellaneous	Field Return.		
War Diary	Chelers	01/11/1916	02/11/1916
War Diary	Rebreuviette	03/11/1916	03/11/1916
War Diary	Barly	04/11/1916	04/11/1916
War Diary	Berneuil	05/11/1916	14/11/1916
War Diary	Villers L'Hopital	15/11/1916	15/11/1916
War Diary	Villers L'Hopital	16/11/1916	16/11/1916
War Diary	Bouquemaison	17/11/1916	17/11/1916
War Diary	Sus St Leger	18/11/1916	21/11/1916
War Diary	Doullens	22/11/1916	22/11/1916
War Diary	Berteaucourt	23/11/1916	23/11/1916
War Diary	Pont Remy	24/11/1916	25/11/1916
War Diary	Mouflers	26/11/1916	05/12/1916
War Diary	Camp 124 Sailly Le Sec	11/12/1916	27/12/1916
War Diary	Camp 17 Suzanne	28/12/1916	31/12/1916
Heading	War Diary of 12th Bn Suffolk Regt From 1/1/17 To 31/1/17 (Volume 8)		
Miscellaneous			
War Diary	Bouchavesnes	01/01/1917	04/01/1917
War Diary	Camp 23.	05/01/1917	08/01/1917
War Diary	Camp 17	09/01/1917	12/01/1917
War Diary	Rancourt.	13/01/1917	22/01/1917
War Diary	Camp 17	23/01/1917	24/01/1917
War Diary	Camp B. Chipilly	25/01/1917	27/01/1917
War Diary	Belair.	28/01/1917	31/01/1917
Miscellaneous	Field Return.		
Miscellaneous	For Information of the A.G's Office at the Base.		
Heading	War Diary of 12th Bn. Suffolk Regt From Feb 1st To Feb. 28th Vol 9		
War Diary	Belair	01/02/1917	01/02/1917
War Diary	Camp.	02/02/1917	09/02/1917
War Diary	Camp 111	10/02/1917	22/02/1917
War Diary	Maurepas	23/02/1917	24/02/1917
War Diary	Rancourt	25/02/1917	28/02/1917
War Diary	Camp 165	01/03/1917	01/03/1917
War Diary	Maurepas	02/03/1917	03/03/1917
War Diary	Rancourt	04/03/1917	07/03/1917
War Diary	Pc. Bonnett	08/03/1917	08/03/1917
War Diary	Camp 17	09/03/1917	15/03/1917
War Diary	Pc Merton	16/03/1917	18/03/1917
War Diary	Peronne	19/03/1917	20/03/1917
War Diary	Mt St Quinton	21/03/1917	24/03/1917
War Diary	Camp at I.8.G.	25/03/1917	31/03/1917
Heading	War Diary of 12th Bn Suffolk Regt From April 1st 1917 To April 30th 1917 Volume XI		
Miscellaneous			
Miscellaneous	Field Return.		
Miscellaneous			
War Diary	Mt St Quinton	01/04/1917	01/04/1917
War Diary	I.9.C. 4.5. Sheet 62 CNW	02/04/1917	05/04/1917
War Diary	Fins V 12.b.8.2. Sheet 57c SE	07/04/1917	10/04/1917
War Diary	Desartwood WI C 2-2 Sheet 57 C SE	11/04/1917	13/04/1917

War Diary	Queens Cross Q 28 d 3-2 Sheet 57c SE.	14/04/1917	17/04/1917
War Diary	Etricourt Q 8 a 8-3 Sheet 57 CSE	18/04/1917	25/04/1917
War Diary	Queens Cross	26/04/1917	30/04/1917
Miscellaneous			
Miscellaneous	Field Return.		
Miscellaneous			
War Diary	Area Villers Plovich R 13. Map 57 C.S.E.	01/05/1917	06/05/1917
War Diary	Desart Wood	07/05/1917	08/05/1917
War Diary	Map. 57 CSE	08/05/1917	08/05/1917
War Diary	Desart Wood	09/05/1917	12/05/1917
War Diary	Heudecourt	13/05/1917	14/05/1917
War Diary	Villers Guislain	15/05/1917	23/05/1917
War Diary	Dessart Wood	24/05/1917	26/05/1917
War Diary	Gouzeaucourt Area	27/05/1917	31/05/1917
Miscellaneous	Operation Orders By Lieut Col. T. Eardley-Wilmot., D.S.O. Commanding Battalion Suffolk Regiment. Appendix I		
Miscellaneous	40th Division. List of N.C.O.S. And Men Awarded The Military Medal. Appendix II		
Map	Gonnelieu Salient		
Map			
War Diary	Villers Plouich Sector Q. 29.6. 2.2. Map 57.C.SE	01/06/1917	03/06/1917
War Diary	Dessart Wood W 2 a Map 57 C.SE	04/06/1917	11/06/1917
War Diary	Gonnelieu	12/06/1917	19/06/1917
War Diary	W 4.a. 1.4.	20/06/1917	21/06/1917
War Diary	W 6.d.6.5.	22/06/1917	27/06/1917
War Diary	Sorel	28/06/1917	30/06/1917
Miscellaneous	Operation Orders By Lieut Col. T. Eardley-Wilmot. D.S.O., Commanding Battalion Suffolk Regiment.	02/06/1917	02/06/1917
Miscellaneous	Operation Orders By Lieut. Col. T. Eardley-Wilmot, D.S.O., Commanding Battalion Suffolk Regiment.	18/06/1917	18/06/1917
Miscellaneous	Operation Orders By Lieut. Col. T. Eardley-Wilmot, D.S.O., Commdg. 12th Bn. Suffolk Regiment.	26/06/1917	26/06/1917
Miscellaneous	Appendix O		
Heading	War Diary of 12th Bn Suffolk Regt From 1/7/17 To 31/7/17 (Volume 14)		
Miscellaneous			
Miscellaneous	Field Return.		
Heading	War Diary of 12th Bn Suffolk Regt From 1/7/17 To 31/7/17 (Volume 14)		
War Diary	Map Refs Sheet 57.C. S.E. Sorel	01/07/1917	02/07/1917
War Diary	Villers Guislain	03/07/1917	18/07/1917
War Diary	Vaucelette Farm.	19/07/1917	25/07/1917
War Diary	Villers Guislain	26/07/1917	31/07/1917
Miscellaneous	Operation Orders by Major L. Lloyd. Commdg. 12th. Bn. Suffolk Regiment. Appendix 1	01/07/1917	01/07/1917
Miscellaneous	Operation Orders By Lieut. Col. T. Eardley-Wilmot, D.S.O. Commdg 12th. Bn. Suffolk Regiment. Appendix 2	10/07/1917	10/07/1917
Miscellaneous	Operation Orders By Lieut. Col. T. Eardley-Wilmot, D.S.O. Commanding 12th. Bn. Suffolk Regiment. Appendix 3	17/07/1917	17/07/1917
Miscellaneous			
Miscellaneous	Battalion Orders By Lieut. Col. T. Eardley-Wilmot", D.S.O. Commanding Bn. Suffolk Regiment.	22/07/1917	22/07/1917

Miscellaneous	Operation Orders By Lieut. Col. T. Eardley-Wilmot, D.S.O. Commdg 12th Bn. Suffolk Regiment. Appendix 5	24/07/1917	24/07/1917
Miscellaneous Heading	War Diary of 12th Bn Suffolk Regt From 1/8/17 To 31/8/17 (Volume 15)		
Miscellaneous			
War Diary	Villers Guislain	01/08/1917	01/08/1917
War Diary	Gonnelieu	02/08/1917	11/08/1917
War Diary	Vaucellette Farm	12/08/1917	19/08/1917
War Diary	Gonnelieu	20/08/1917	27/08/1917
War Diary	Vaucelette Farm	28/08/1917	31/08/1917
Miscellaneous	Defence Scheme. Left Battalion-121st Infantry Brigade Appendix A	03/08/1917	03/08/1917
Miscellaneous	Operation Orders by Lieut. Col. T. Eardley-Wilmot, D.S.O., Commdg. 12th Bn. Suffolk Regiment. Appendix I	01/08/1917	01/08/1917
Miscellaneous	Operation Orders by Lieut. Col, T. Eardley-Wilmot, D.S.O., Commdg. 12th Bn. Suffolk Regiment. Appendix 2	02/08/1917	02/08/1917
Miscellaneous	Operation Orders By Lieut. Col, T. Eardley-Wilmot, D.S.O., Commanding 12th Bn. Suffolk Regt. Appendix 3	10/08/1917	10/08/1917
Miscellaneous			
Miscellaneous	Operation Orders by Lieut Col T. Eardley-Wilmot, D.S.O. Commdg 12th Bn Suffolk Regt. Appendix 4	14/08/1917	14/08/1917
Miscellaneous			
Miscellaneous	Operation Orders by Lieut Col T. Eardley-Wilmot, D.S.O. Commanding 12th Bn. Suffolk Regt Appendix 5	18/08/1917	18/08/1917
Miscellaneous	Operation Orders by Lieut Col T. Eardley-Wilmot, D.S.O. Commdg 12th Bn. Suffolk Regt Appendix 6	26/08/1917	26/08/1917
Miscellaneous	Operation Orders by Lieut Col T. Eardley-Wilmot, Commdg 12th Bn. Suffolk Regt. Appendix 7	31/08/1917	31/08/1917
Miscellaneous			
Miscellaneous	Field Return.		
Heading	War Diary of 12th Bn Suffolk From 1/9/17 To 30/9/17 (Volume 16)		
Miscellaneous			
War Diary	Gonnelieu	01/09/1917	12/09/1917
War Diary	Vaucelette Farm	13/09/1917	16/09/1917
War Diary	Gonnelieu	17/09/1917	19/09/1917
War Diary	Vaucelette Farm	20/09/1917	23/09/1917
War Diary	Gonnelieu	24/09/1917	30/09/1917
Miscellaneous	Operation Orders by Major T. Miskin. Commdg. 12th Bn. Suffolk Regt. Appendix I	31/08/1917	31/08/1917
Miscellaneous	Operation Orders by Major T. Miskin. Commdg. 12th Bn. Suffolk Regt. Appendix II.	11/09/1917	11/09/1917
Miscellaneous	Operation Orders by Lieut Col. T. Eardley Wilmot D.S.O. Commdg. 12th Bn. Suffolk Regt. Appendix 3	16/09/1917	16/09/1917
Miscellaneous	Operation Orders by Lieut. Col. T. Eardley-Wilmot, D.S.O. Commdg 12th Bn Suffolk Regt. Appendix 4	18/09/1917	18/09/1917
Miscellaneous	Operation Orders by Lieut. Col. T. Eardley-Wilmot, D.S.O. Commdg 12th Bn. Suffolk Regt. Appendix 5	23/09/1917	23/09/1917

Miscellaneous	Operation Orders by Lieutenant-Colonel T. Eardley-Wilmot, D.S.O., Commanding 12th. Bn. Suffolk Regiment.	21/09/1917	21/09/1917
Miscellaneous	No. 1 Party.		
Miscellaneous	No. 2 Party.		
Miscellaneous	No. 3 Party Supports.		
Miscellaneous	No. 4 Party.		
Miscellaneous	No. 5 Party.		
Miscellaneous	No. 6 Part. Supports.		
Miscellaneous	Appendix A		
Miscellaneous	Appendix B		
Miscellaneous	Field Return.		
Miscellaneous			
Heading	War Diary of 12th Bn. Suffolk Regt From 1/10/17 To 31/10/17 (Volume 17)		
Miscellaneous			
War Diary	Gonnelieu.	01/10/1917	05/10/1917
War Diary	Vaucellette Farm	06/10/1917	09/10/1917
War Diary	Sorel	10/10/1917	10/10/1917
War Diary	Peronne	11/10/1917	11/10/1917
War Diary	Bavincourt Map. Sic.	12/10/1917	31/10/1917
Miscellaneous			
Miscellaneous	Field Return.		
Miscellaneous			
Heading	War Diary of 12th Bn Suffolk Regt. from Nov 1st To Nov. 31st (Volume 18)		
Miscellaneous			
Miscellaneous	Field Return.		
Miscellaneous			
War Diary	Sus St Leger	01/11/1917	16/11/1917
War Diary	Bavincourt	16/11/1917	17/11/1917
War Diary	Achiet Le Petit	18/11/1917	19/11/1917
War Diary	Rocquigny	20/11/1917	21/11/1917
War Diary	Beaumetz Lez Cambrai	22/11/1917	22/11/1917
War Diary	Bourlon	23/11/1917	25/11/1917
War Diary	Hindenburg Line	26/11/1917	26/11/1917
War Diary	Bavincourt	27/11/1917	27/11/1917
War Diary	Baillelmont	28/11/1917	30/11/1917
War Diary	Lens II Bailleumont	01/12/1917	01/12/1917
War Diary	Hamelincourt	02/12/1917	02/12/1917
War Diary	Tunnel Trench U 7d to U 14.a.	03/12/1917	10/12/1917
War Diary	Hamelincourt	11/12/1917	17/12/1917
War Diary	Croisilles	18/12/1917	24/12/1917
War Diary	Hamelincourt	25/12/1917	31/12/1917
Miscellaneous	Minor Operations Enemy attach on 12 Suff. R., 121 Bde, 40 Div. on 5 Jany 1918		
War Diary	Map Lens II Ecoust	01/01/1918	04/01/1918
War Diary	Bullecourt	05/01/1918	08/01/1918
War Diary	Mory	09/01/1918	12/01/1918
War Diary	Bullecourt	13/01/1918	16/01/1918
War Diary	Ecoust	17/01/1918	20/01/1918
War Diary	Bullecourt	21/01/1918	24/01/1918
War Diary	Mory	25/01/1918	28/01/1918
War Diary	Bullecourt	29/01/1918	31/01/1918
War Diary	Immediate Awards	31/01/1918	31/01/1918

Heading	War Diary of 12th Bn. Suffolk Regt From Jan 1st 1918. To Jan 31st 1918 (Volume 20)		
Miscellaneous			
Miscellaneous	Preliminary Report on Enemy attack on 12th Suffolks (40th Division) on the moring of January 5th.	06/01/1918	06/01/1918
Miscellaneous	Field Return.		
Miscellaneous			
Heading	War Diary For 12th Bn Suffolk Regt from 1/2/18 To 28/1/18 Volume 21		
Miscellaneous			
War Diary	Bullecourt	01/02/1918	01/02/1918
War Diary	Ecoust	02/02/1918	06/02/1918
War Diary	Bullecourt	08/02/1918	12/02/1918
War Diary	Mory	13/02/1918	13/02/1918
War Diary	Hamelincourt	14/02/1918	27/02/1918
War Diary	Bailleulmont	28/02/1918	28/02/1918
Miscellaneous	12th Bn Suffolk Rgt		
Miscellaneous	Officer-Reinforcements during month		
Heading	40th Division. 121st Infantry Brigade. War Diary 12th Battalion The Suffolk Regiment March 1918 Attached Report On Operations 21st-26th		
War Diary	Map Lens. II Bailleulmont	01/03/1918	12/03/1918
War Diary	Blairville	13/03/1918	21/03/1918
War Diary	In action Corps	21/03/1918	22/03/1918
War Diary	Army Lines	23/03/1918	25/03/1918
War Diary	Bienvillers	26/03/1918	26/03/1918
War Diary	Sus. St. Leger.	27/03/1918	29/03/1918
War Diary	Bailleul-Aux-Cornailles	30/03/1918	30/03/1918
War Diary	Neuf Berquin.	31/03/1918	31/03/1918
Miscellaneous	Account of Action 21th/26th March 1918		
Miscellaneous	2/6 Leicesters		
Miscellaneous			
Miscellaneous	For 2nd March, 1918		
Heading	40th Division. 121st Infantry Brigade. War Diary 12th Battalion The Suffolk Regiment. April 1918 Narrative of Operations 9th-13th April.		
War Diary	Bois Grenier Sector	01/04/1918	05/04/1918
War Diary	Fleurbaix	06/04/1918	09/04/1918
War Diary	Bavinchove	13/04/1918	13/04/1918
War Diary	St Omer.	14/04/1918	20/04/1918
War Diary	Bavinchove	21/04/1918	21/04/1918
War Diary	Herzeele	22/04/1918	23/04/1918
War Diary	Rweld	24/04/1918	27/04/1918
War Diary	Proven	28/04/1918	30/04/1918
Miscellaneous	Narrative Of Operations Of 12th Suffolks From 9th/13th April, 1918.	13/04/1918	13/04/1918
Miscellaneous	Strength For 27th April 1918		
Miscellaneous	Officers Other Ranks.		
War Diary	Proven	01/05/1918	01/05/1918
War Diary	Terdeghem.	02/05/1918	02/05/1918
War Diary	Klinderbelk	03/05/1918	17/05/1918
War Diary	Sercus	18/05/1918	29/05/1918
War Diary	Nordpeene	30/05/1918	31/05/1918

WO95/2616/1

40TH DIVISION
121ST INFY BDE

12TH BN SUFFOLK REGT

JUN 1916 - MAY 1918

FROM U.K.
TO 14 DIV, 43 BDE

No 1. Confidential.

WAR DIARY of 12th Bn Suffolk Regiment.
INTELLIGENCE SUMMARY
(Erase heading not required.)

XI Vol I

Army Form C. 2118

From May 27th 1916 to June 30th 1916

Place	Date	Hour	Summary of Events and Information	Remarks and references to Appendices
PIRBRIGHT	27.5.16	6 am	Battalion Mobilized at PIRBRIGHT Camp, Surrey.	
"	4.6.16	12 o'c	Battalion entrained at BROOKWOOD Railway Station in two parties & proceeded to SOUTHAMPTON.	
SOUTHAMPTON	5.6.16	6 pm	Battalion Embarked at SOUTHAMPTON	
LE HAVRE	6.6.16	4 am	Arrived LE HAVRE. Disembarked 8 am, & proceeded to Rest Camp LE HAVRE	
"	6.6.16	1 pm	Entrained at LE HAVRE Railway Station	
LILLERS	7.6.16	12 noon	Detrained at LILLERS* & proceeded to Billet	*Ref map FRANCE Sheet 36 A.20.b scale 1/40,000
CHOCQUES & LABEUVRIERE	9.6.16	1 pm	Proceeded by route march to CHOCQUES#, for special training in bombing, Attack, digging & repairing Trenches, & musketry. A special Gas Course was undergone at 12th Divisional School LABEUVRIERE#. Billets could not be found for the whole Battalion at CHOCQUES#. "A" & "B" Companies therefore took over the available billets at CHOCQUES#. Head Quarters & "C" & "D" Companies proceeded to the village of LABEUVRIERE & billeted there	#Ref map FRANCE Sheet 36 B. 3.23 Edition scale 1/40000
LILLERS	12.6.16	6 am	Returned by route march to billets at LILLERS*	
"	17.6.16		4 other ranks wounded by accidental Grenade explosion, 12th Divisional School LABEUVRIERE#, 1 since died in Hospital	
BARLIN	19.6.16	10 am	Proceeded by route march to BARLIN#, arriving at billet at 12.15 pm	
"	21.6.16	5.20 pm	Capt C.A. Nisbet Killed & 1 man wounded by accidental Grenade explosion.	
" to CALONNE	24.6.16 to 28th	9.30 am	The Battalion moved from BARLIN# by route march & proceeded to take up position in the trenches in the CALONNE° section. A. & B. Companies arrived in the trenches at 3 pm & were attached to the 1st Bn. Black Watch for instruction, on man to man & Platoon basis. On June 26th the Black Watch were relieved by the 1st Camerons. C. & D. Companies were attached to the 10th Gloucesters & went to the Trenches at 5 am 26th June for instruction on man to man & Platoon basis. No particular incident of note occurred during the period the Battalion was in the Trenches, except that own Artillery was very active occasionally, & hostile Artillery & T.M. shelled our front & support lines intermittently. All ranks gained experience & derived much benefit from their 4 days instruction. The Casualties during the 4 days the Battalion was in the Trenches totalled 15, wounded, 1 Killed & 1 missing. Casualties almost without exception were the result of Artillery fire & T.M.s. — The behaviour of all Ranks, under fire for the first time was most [satisfactory?]. The Battalion left the Trenches on the 28th June & marched to billets at BARLIN#	°Ref map FRANCE Sheet 36 C Edition scale 1/40000.

Confidential.

WAR DIARY.

of

12th (S) Battalion Suffolk Regiment.

from 1st July, 1916 to 31st July, 1916.

Original.

40 July
12 Suffolk
V & Q

Volume II

Sheet I

WAR DIARY or ~~INTELLIGENCE SUMMARY~~

(Erase heading not required.)

12th Bn Suffolk Regt.
From July 1st to 31st 1916.

Army Form C. 2118.

Instructions regarding War Diaries and Intelligence Summaries are contained in F. S. Regs., Part II. and the Staff Manual respectively. Title pages will be prepared in manuscript.

Place	Date	Hour	Summary of Events and Information	Remarks and references to Appendices
BARLIN	1.7.16		Battalion in rest billets. AWG	
"	2.7.16	6.30 p.m	The Battalion moved from BARLIN and relieved the 11th Bn. Royal Sussex Regiment, which was in support. AWG	
MAROC	3.7.16	9 a.m.	The Battalion relieved the 8th Bn. Royal North Lancashire Regt. who were holding the Left Sub-section, MAROC Section. Three Companies were in the Front Line, finding their own supports, with one company in support. The Battalion Bombers were on duty at the DOUBLE CRASSIER. AWG	
"	4.7.16			
"	5.7.16		The Battalion was relieved at 6.30 p.m by 21st. Bn. Middlesex Regt., and went into reserve in billets at NORTH MAROC.	
"			During the period the Battalion was doing duty in the trenches, there were no important occurences.	
			Whilst on duty in the Northern Crassier Sap Head on the night of July 3rd, No. 24586 Lance-Corpl. A. C. Handy, a bomber, heard a German Patrol advancing towards our Sap-head. He at once crawled over the Sap-head, threw bombs at the patrol, forcing them to retire, and returned to our lines safely. He acted entirely on his own initiative and went out alone. For this plucky act, Lance-Corpl. Handy was awarded the Military Medal.	

WAR DIARY
or
INTELLIGENCE SUMMARY

Army Form C. 2118.

Place	Date	Hour	Summary of Events and Information	Remarks and references to Appendices
MAROC			the first honour gained by the 46th Division since it landed in France. The Battalion gained a lot of useful experience in mixing under fire, volunteering and gaining information. The total casualties in the Battalion for this period were: Other Ranks 2 killed and 14 wounded. OMS	
"	4.7.16	9am	The Battalion again moved into the trenches and occupied the right sub-section above section relieving the 20th Bav. of Liffstein Regt. Three companies were in the front line with one company in support. Things were quiet and a lot of useful work was done improving trenches and strengthening our wire. OMS	
"	8.7.16		In the early hours of Saturday morning, at about 3.15 a Jewitt was wounded in the shoulder by an enemy sniper while out with a Patrol. Saturday was very quiet on our whole front. The night was marked by a very heavy bombardment of the enemy lines on our extreme right. In our own section the machine guns were active. OMS	
"	9.7.16		Sunday was again very quiet. At night our artillery showed some activity, whilst machine guns fired on enemy sap and front line. Mining and working parties were engaged during the night. No casualties occurred. OMS	

WAR DIARY or INTELLIGENCE SUMMARY

Army Form C. 2118

Sheet III

Instructions regarding War Diaries and Intelligence Summaries are contained in F. S. Regs., Part II. and the Staff Manual respectively. Title Pages will be prepared in manuscript.

(Erase heading not required.)

Place	Date	Hour	Summary of Events and Information	Remarks and references to Appendices
MAROC	10.7.16		Monday the situation was normal. Working parties were again busy. AMcG	
"	11.7.16		During Tuesday morning the Battalion was relieved by the 13th Bn. East Surrey Regt. and proceeded to rest billets at LES BREBIS. During this period in the trenches, the casualties were: 2/Lieut. R.J.C. Jewitt wounded, O.R. 1 killed and 2 wounded. AMcG	
LES BREBIS	12.7.16 13.7.16 14.7.16 15.7.16 16.7.16		The Battalion was in rest billets at LES BREBIS on July 12th, 13th, 14th, 15th and 16th. During this period fatigues and working parties were found for the Brigade. AMcG	
MAROC	17.7.16		The Battalion proceeded to Reserve Billets in NORTH MAROC in the evening of July 17th as Brigade reserve. AMcG	
"	18.7.16		Working parties proceeded to the front line. Working parties were found for battalions of the Brigade AMcG	
"	19.7.16 20.7.16		in Front Line System. AMcG	
"	21.7.16		Still in Reserve billets. AMcG	
"	22.7.16		The Battalion moved from reserve at MAROC to No. 3 Sub-section of the LOOS Section, taking over the new position about 2 a.m. Map Reference M/6/B/6½/3½ Sheet 36c SW to 4/31/A/6/3 Sheet 36c N.W.	

WAR DIARY
or
INTELLIGENCE SUMMARY

Army Form C. 2118

Place	Date	Hour	Summary of Events and Information	Remarks and references to Appendices
AUTHUILLE	22.7.16		The Battalions on our right and left respectively were the 21st Middlesex, no 8th Bn. and the 2nd Manchester Regiment in Bn. 6/13th Royal Scots Rifles. Our	
	23.7.16		The enemy bombarded our front with Rifle Grenades and Canal Torpedoes intermittently during the day. In the course of this, 2/Lieut R.W. Robinson was wounded, 3 O.R. killed and 5 O.R. wounded.	Quiet
	24.7.16		Generally quiet.	Quiet
	25.7.16		Spasmodic shelling with H.E. and the usual Rifle Grenades and Canal Torpedoes. In return we replied with Rifle Grenades and Trench Howitzers.	Quiet
	26.7.16		About 2.30 a.m. an aeroplane turns silenced the enemy aeroplane guns. During the day we were dealt with Rifle Grenades, Trench Howitzers and artillery. About 5.35 p.m. some 40 to 5.9 shells were fired on our front and Support lines, and again at 6.15 3 salvoes of 4 guns each 4th-8th were fired at the same point.	Quiet
	27.7.16		Much damage was done to our parapets by enemy Grenades and artillery. At night we bombarded the enemy line with Rifle Grenades, Heavy guns and Trench Howitzers, to which they retaliated weakly.	Quiet

WAR DIARY or INTELLIGENCE SUMMARY

Army Form C. 2118

Sheet V

Place	Date	Hour	Summary of Events and Information	Remarks and references to Appendices
LOOS	28.7.16		The usual duals with Rifle Grenades, Trench Mortars and Artillery. Our trenches and saps were knocked about. At midnight a party of the enemy approached and commenced throwing Hand Grenades but were immediately dispersed by rifle fire. AWC	
"	29.7.16		Quieter. We shelled Cameron Crater with Stokes Guns. AWC	
"	30.7.16		Rifle Grenades and Trench Mortars were fairly active. Later in the day, the enemy Rifle Grenades were silenced by our retaliation. AWC	
"	31.7.16		Fairly quiet on our whole front. 2/Lieut D. G. Carr was wounded. AWC	

Rhodgate Lt Col
Comdg 12th Bn
1-8-16 Suffolk Regt

Army Form W. 3091.

Cover for Documents.

Nature of Enclosures.

Original Copy

Confidential

WAR DIARY
of
15th (S) Bn SUFFOLK REGT:

from Aug 1st 1916 to Aug 31st 1916

Volume 3

Notes, or Letters written.

Sheet 1

WAR DIARY
INTELLIGENCE SUMMARY
(Erase heading not required.)

12th Battalion Suffolk Regt.

Army Form C. 2118.

Place	Date	Hour	Summary of Events and Information	Remarks and references to Appendices
LOOS	Aug 1st		Generally quiet, with occasional Rifle Grenade activity on both sides. AMC	
"	2nd		Our artillery active at 6.45 p.m. At 11.5 p.m. the enemy blew up a small Camouflet in No 1. Gallery, by Cameron Alley. Their charge, however, was not strong enough to explode ours, and only slight damage was done to our gallery. No damage was done to our trenches. AMC	
"	3rd		At 1 a.m. the enemy bombarded us heavily with Rifle Grenades, aerial Torpedoes, and Trench Mortars. We replied with Rifle Grenades and Stoke Guns on the CAMERON MOUNDS. The enemy ceased at 1.30 a.m. Damage done very slight. AMC An enemy aeroplane dropped a bomb close to Battalion Headquarters at 6.45 p.m. doing no damage.	
"	4th		At 1.15 a.m. we carried out a raid on CAMERON and GORDON CRATERS and the WHITE MOUND between GORDON and SEAFORTH CRATERS. All details were arranged by CAPT. J.F. PLUNKETT, "D" Company. The three parties were commanded by 2/LIEUT H.A. REDDING, LIEUT. C.H. ROLPH and SERGT. C. WILLS respectively. All reached their objectives without casualties. The party under 2/LIEUT. H.A. REDDING succeeded in their object i.e. to blow up an enemy mine shaft. They also destroyed a deep dug-out in the sap leading to Crater. Total casualties, three wounded. AMC	

WAR DIARY
or
INTELLIGENCE SUMMARY.

Army Form C. 2118.

15th B. Suffolk Regt.

Sheet 7

Place	Date	Hour	Summary of Events and Information	Remarks and references to Appendices
1916				
LOOS	August		The Bat. Casualties during the tour of duty amounted to:- 2 Officers wounded OR's 5 killed 1 Wounded. 92 Reinforcements. The Bat. moved into Billets in N. MAROC in the evening being relieved in Trenches by H. 150th Brigade. The 12th E. SURREYS took over the place in the line vacated by the Bat.	
N. MAROC	5.6.7.8. Aug.		In billets in N. MAROC. The Batt. found own fatigues.	OWC
"	9		The Batt. moved into Front Billets in LES BREBIS. The 13th & 14th E. SURREYS.	OWC
LES BREBIS	10.11		In LES BREBIS. Found fatigue parties.	OWC
"	12		The Batt. moved into front line trenches in S. MAROC. Major T. EARDLEY WILMOT in Command. Bat. left at 8am from 14th HLI. O.R. 458 front south 3 Offs. 9 Vickers Maxim Mg. 26th & 8 Stokes. 11.9 Bangalore in the night front.	OWC
S. MAROC	13		On the night of 13/13 2/Lt SHAW was hit in the knee by a Rifle Grenade whilst out on Patrol. At 11.55 p.m. 13 Aust our Artillery opened a heavy bombardment on the Enemy line continued until 1 a.m. 13th. 96 Ammunition of this day fairly Quiet except odd rev rifle fire. The enemy used over a fair Casual trajects + Rifle Grenades.	OWC
	14		The enemy used over large number of Rifle Grenade + Casual trajects tosses 8.30 to 9 am.	

Sheet 3. **WAR DIARY** 12th Bn Suffolk Regt Army Form C. 2118.
or
INTELLIGENCE SUMMARY.
(Erase heading not required.)

Instructions regarding War Diaries and Intelligence Summaries are contained in F. S. Regs., Part II. and the Staff Manual respectively. Title pages will be prepared in manuscript.

Place	Date	Hour	Summary of Events and Information	Remarks and references to Appendices
	14		We retaliated with Stokes Guns & the enemy ceased fire. From 1pm to 4pm the enemy bombarded our Communication & Support trenches with Artillery & Trench Mortars & again at 6.45pm heavily bombarded our right with Aerial Torpedoes & Rifle Grenades. We replied with Stokes Guns & Rifle Grenades. About 9.30pm the enemy shelled our right but were quickly silenced by our Artillery. AWC	
	15		About m.n. 14/15 Aug we fired a large number of Rifle Grenades to which the enemy replied very weakly. At 8.30am the enemy blew in a part of our Support line with H.E. Shell. This was quickly repaired. Between 12 m.n. & 4 am & again between 10 am & 12 noon the enemy shelled our Support & Communication Trenches. Slight damage was done & quickly repaired. AWC	
	16.		Between 1.30 & 2 am we fired nearly 200 Rifle Grenades on to the enemy line to which we received little or no reply. Enemy bombarded our line with Rifle Grenades & Aerial Torpedoes between 8.30 & 10 am. We effectively replied with Stokes Guns & Rifle Grenades. About 9.15 pm the enemy replied to our Stokes Gun fire with Rifle Grenades & Aerial Torpedoes causing slight damage to our Trenches AWC	
	17		An enemy wiring party was dispersed by our fire at 2.30 am. Remainder of the day was generally quiet except for occasional Rifle Grenades & Trench Mortars AWC	

WAR DIARY
or
INTELLIGENCE SUMMARY

Army Form C. 2118.

12th & 13th Suffolk Regt.

Sept. 14

Place	Date	Hour	Summary of Events and Information	Remarks and references to Appendices
	Aug 3/4			
	18		Fairly quiet. Recovered rifle Equipment & Small repairs.	OWC
	19		During the day quiet. At night about 10.15 pm D & B Companies carried out Raid on the enemy trenches. A Report made by 2/Lt A.G. Burrows length in	See Appendix A to annex
			2/Lt A.G. Burrows was wounded. OWC Casualties during the two Raids: 1 Officer wounded, 2 Men wounded.	
NMAROC	20		The Batt moved into Reserve Billets in NMAROC	OWC 1 Officer wounded 2
	21		In Reserve Billets. Found working parties	OWC
	22		do do	OWC
	23		do do	OWC
	24		do do	OWC
	25		do do	OWC
	26		do do	OWC
	27		Two Companies went into the front line in SMAROC + 2 other Platoons SMAROC.	
	28		moved the 12 EPs. The remaining 6 Platoons continue in NMAROC OWC. The remainder of the Batt moved into trenches in SMAROC, relieving one Company of the 50th Middlesex Regt. The 19th M Regt on our Right & left were	
			11 & 13 King Own R.L + 2/10th Middlesex respectively OWC	

Sheet 5
WAR DIARY
INTELLIGENCE SUMMARY
12th Bn Suffolk Regt.

Place	Date	Hour	Summary of Events and Information	Remarks and references to Appendices
S MAROC	1916 Aug. 29		Very quiet. Heavy thunder storm at 4 pm. Very heavy rain from then onwards doing much damage to trenches AWC	
	30.		Again very quiet generally. No activity on either side. The trenches again fell in at various places owing to heavy rain AWC	
	31.		At 4.45 a.m. we blew a mine at M 4/d/15750 just S of the S. CRASSIER on the left of our line. We at the same time bombarded the enemy front & support line with Artillery, Trench Mortars, & Rifle Grenades. No reply from the enemy. Remainder of the day very quiet AWC	

T. Lawley Lieut Col

WAR DIARY
or
INTELLIGENCE SUMMARY

Army Form C. 2118.

15th S. Staffs Regt.

Appendix "A"

At about 10.15 p.m. on the 19th August 1916 whilst the B/n were in SMALOC T.27 Coy carried out a raid on the enemy trench. The party under 2/Lt A.G. BURROWS crossed No mans land to the German wire + got through a gap in the first line wire + then had to crawl under the wire just in front of their trench. 2/Lt A.G. BURROWS closely followed by 6.3720 Pte F.E.W. LC + 8.2033 Pte LANE W jumped into the trench + almost immediately came a German. 2/Lt A. G. led Gunn + the German turned + ran. 2/Lt A.G. BURROWS following him. After a few yards the German turned – Pte. about 3 yds away when he saw another German advancing on a few off when about 3 yds away when he saw another German advancing on a few off the fired at him. 2/Lt A.G. BURROWS then caught hold of his rifle and his left hand + pulled him off the firestep by his neck. After a struggle he succeeded in getting him along the trench — with the help of Pte F.E.W. LANE got him over the H.P. + brought him back to our lines. 2/Lt Having all the 2/Lt A.G. BURROWS was wounded 4 times in the leg. Pte of this he continued before entering the German trench.

AWB
AWB

Confidential

Vol 4

WAR DIARY
of 12th Bn SUFFOLK REGT.

From Sept. 1st 1916 To Sept. 30th 1916.

Volume IV

Original Copy

			WAR DIARY	Army Form C. 2118.

Instructions regarding War Diaries and Intelligence Summaries are contained in F. S. Regs., Part II. and the Staff Manual respectively. Title pages will be prepared in manuscript.

Sheet 1

WAR DIARY
or
INTELLIGENCE SUMMARY.
(Erase heading not required.)

12th/16th Suffolk Regt

Place	Date	Hour	Summary of Events and Information	Remarks and references to Appendices
	1916			
S. MAROC	1/9/16	6.15 am	The Batt. moved out of the Front Line into Reserve Billets in S. MAROC.	
			Total Casualties while in this Sector 6. O.R. Wounded.	amc
	2/9/16		Reserve Billets S. MAROC	amc
	3/9/16		" " "	amc
	4/9/16		" " "	amc
	5/9/16		" " " Moved to LES BREBIS at 8 pm	amc
LES BREBIS	6/9/16		Brigade in Reserve Billets. Found fatigue parties	amc
	7/9/16		" " " " " " "	amc
	8/9/16		" " " " " " "	amc
	9/9/16		" " " " " " "	amc
	10/9/16		" " " Lewis Guns moved into Front Line at LOOS	amc
LOOS	11/9/16		Took over left Sub. sector from 18th Welch. 21st Middlesex on our right + R.W.S	
			76th Brigade on our Left	amc
	12/9/16		Situation quiet. Few Rifle Grenades exchanged. No enemy artillery	amc
	13/9/16		A few enemy shells, "whizz bangs". In the afternoon a fairly lively exchange of Rifle	
			Grenades. Later we opened fire with Rifle Grenades & Stokes Guns, no enemy retaliation	

T2134. Wt. W708—776. 500000. 4/15. Sir J. C. & S.

Sheet II

WAR DIARY or INTELLIGENCE SUMMARY.

12th Bn Suffolk Regt

Army Form C. 2118.

Place	Date	Hour	Summary of Events and Information	Remarks and references to Appendices
LOOS.	13/9/16	8.30pm	We manned parapet & fired a burst of 10 rounds rapid Rifle, Rifle Grenade & Stokes Gun fire. The Enemy did not man his parapets. Retaliation silenced by our Stokes Guns	AWC
	14/9/16	4 am	We fired a number of Rifle Grenades to which Enemy replied weakly	AWC
	15/9/16		Usual exchange of Rifle Grenades, otherwise quiet especially throughout the night	AWC
	16/9/16		Quiet. A few Rifle Grenades exchanged. During the morning the Enemy fired a few small shells at SEAFORTH CRATER doing no damage. We replied with Shrapnel on his front line	AWC
	17/9/16		Few Arial torpedoes & Rifle Grenades. We replied with Rifle Grenades & Trench Mortars. Our Lewis Guns silenced Enemy M.G. near GORDON CRATER at 9.30pm	AWC
	18/9/16		Generally quiet. At 6.45pm we blew two mines at SEAFORTH CRATER which we at once consolidated. Enemy replied to our Artillery with M.Gs & Rifle Grenades only.	AWC
	19/9/16		The Batt. was relieved by 20th Middlesex. We taking over in VILLAGE LINES. Total Casualties during this tour of duty O.R. 6 Killed 30 wounded.	AWC AWC

WAR DIARY or INTELLIGENCE SUMMARY

Sheet III
1/5th Stafford Regt.
Army Form C. 2118.

Place	Date	Hour	Summary of Events and Information	Remarks and references to Appendices
Loos	20/9/16		In Brigade Support in VILLAGE LINE.	qme
	21/9/16		" " " " " " "	qme
	22/9/16		" " " " " " "	qme
	23/9/16		" " " " " " "	qme
N MAROC	23/9/16		Moved to N MAROC taking over from 3rd N. Staffords.	qme
	24/9/16		In N MAROC in Brigade Support	qme
	25/9/16		"G." Coy. Relieved from Right flank at 10.2 pm. Harrod ambulance arrived at 10.10 pm.	qme
xxxx	26/9/16		In N MAROC in Brigade Support	qme
Loos	27/9/16		Moved to left Sub sector LOOS relieving 3rd N.Staffs. On our right flank our 3rd N.Staffs on our left 11th King's Own. Generally quiet.	qme
	28/9/16		A few heavy Trench Mortars fell on us on Support line. There were rumours of an Trench Mortar.	qme
	29/9/16		A little Trench Mortar activity on both Sides.	qme
	30/9/16		Quiet day. Slight Trench Mortar activity at night	qme

T Greenhalgh Lt Col
Comd. 1/5th Staffords Regt.

WAR DIARY
of
2ⁿᵈ B. Suffolk Regt

From Oct 1ˢᵗ 1916.
To Oct 31ˢᵗ 1916.

Original Copy

Vol 5

Perforated Sheet giving detail of personnel and horses wanting to complete, shown on Army Form B. 213.

Number of Report _____

Detail of Wanting to Complete	CAVALRY	R.A.	R.E.	INFANTRY	R.A.M.C.	A.O.C.	A.V.C.
Drivers							
Steam							
Lorry							
Car							
A.S.C.							
R.E.							
R.A.							
Gunners							
Smith Gunners							
Range Takers							
Serjeants							
Corporals							
Farriers							
Shoeing, or Shoeing and Carriage Smiths							
Cold Shoers							
Saddlers or Harness Makers							
Wheelers							
H.T.							
M.T.							
R.A.							
Blacksmiths							
Bricklayers and Masons							
Carpenters and Joiners							
Wood							
Iron } Fitters & Turners (R.E.)							
Fitters							
R.A.							
Wireless							
Plumbers							
Ordinary } Electricians							
W.T.							
Signalmen							
Loco. } Engine Drivers							
Field							
Air Line Men							
Permanent Line Men							
Operators, Telegraph							
Cablemen							
Brigade Section Pioneers							
General-duty Pioneers							
Signallers							
Instrument Repairers							
Motor Cyclists							
Motor Cyclist Artificers							
Telephonists							
Clerks							
Machine Gunners							
Fitters } Armament Artificers							
Range Finders							
Armourers							
Storemen							
Privates							
W.O.'s and N.C.O.'s (by ranks) not included in trade columns							
TOTAL to agree with wanting to complete							
Officers							
Other Ranks							
Horses							
Riding							
Draught							
Heavy Draught							
Pack							

Remarks :—

Signature of Commander. _____

Unit. _____

Formation to which attached. _____

Date of Despatch. _____

[P.T.O.

Only additional information regarding "wanting to complete" is to be entered on this side.

(B 9851) Wt. W15519/M149. 1/16. 1,000,000. J.P.&Co.,Ltd. Forms/B 213/7.

To be made up to and for Sunday in each week.

No. of Report _____ **FIELD RETURN.** Army Form B. 213.

(To be furnished by all arms, services, and departments (except A.S.C. units) to the A. G.'s Office at the Base in accordance with Field Service Regulations, Part II.)

RETURN showing numbers (a) Effective strength of Unit.
(b) Rationed by Unit. _____ at _____ Date.

Detail	Personnel			Animals								Guns, carriages, and limbers and transport vehicles											Remarks
				Horses			Mules									Horsed		Mechanical						
	Officers	Other ranks	Natives	Riding	Draught	Heavy Draught	Pack	Large	Small	Camels	Oxen	Guns, carriages and limbers, showing description	Ammunition wagons and limbers	Machine guns	Aircraft, showing description	4 wheeled	2 wheeled	Motor Cvs.	Tractors	Lorries, showing description	Trucks, showing description	Trailers	Motor Bicycles	Bicycles	
Effective Strength of Unit																									
Details, *by Arms* attached to unit as in War *Establishment :—*																									
Total																									
War Establishment																									
Wanting to complete (Detail of Personnel and Horses below)																									
Surplus																									
*Attached (not to include the details shown above)																									
Civilians :— Employed with the Unit																									
Accompanying the Unit																									
Total Rationed...																									

* In the case of field ambulances, hospitals or depots, the number of patients are to be included here, the names being shown in A. F. A. 36.

_____ Signature of Commander.

_____ Date of Despatch.

For information of the A.G.'s Office at the Base.

Officers and men who have become casuals, been transferred or joined since last report.

Place _____ Date _____

Regtl. Number	Rank	Name	Corps	Nature of casualty, or name of unit from or to which transferred	Date of being struck off or coming on the ration return	Remarks*

* State whether absence is of a permanent or temporary nature, adding, in the case of casuals from wounds or disease, any available information for communication to the relatives.

WAR DIARY ~~INTELLIGENCE SUMMARY~~

Sheet 1   12th Bn Suffolk Regt.

Army Form C. 2118.

(Erase heading not required.)

Place	Date	Hour	Summary of Events and Information	Remarks and references to Appendices
	1916			
LOOS	Oct 1		Quiet day. At night an enemy bombing party were dispersed on our front. Trench Mortar & Rifle Grenade activity during the night. AWC	
	" 2		A raiding party under 2/Lts REDDING & NOBLE entered enemy trenches & killing some brought back 1 wounded prisoner belonging to the 5+1 Regiment. AWC	
	" 3		Trench Mortar activity. An enemy bombing party approached SEAFORTH CRATER & were driven off about 8pm. About 12 m.n. we blew 3 Bangalores under enemy wire clearing a gap about 12' wide. Our patrols attempted to enter & were driven off by the enemy. Lt B.E. PLEDGER & 2/Lt A.V. NOBLE were wounded. AWC	
	" 4		Heavy Trench Mortar fire on both sides during the night. AWC	
	5		Relieved by 20th Middlesex. We took over from them as Batt in Support AWC	
	6		In Support. AWC	
	7		In Support. AWC	
	8		In Support. AWC	
N.MAROC	9		Relieved by 21 Middlesex. We took over from them as Batt in Reserve. Total Casualties during this tour of duty. 2 Officers Wounded. O.R. 2 Killed 21 Wounded AWC	

Sheet II

WAR DIARY
or
INTELLIGENCE SUMMARY.

12th Bn Suffolk Regt

Army Form C. 2118.

Instructions regarding War Diaries and Intelligence Summaries are contained in F. S. Regs., Part II. and the Staff Manual respectively. Title pages will be prepared in manuscript.

(Erase heading not required.)

Place	Date	Hour	Summary of Events and Information	Remarks and references to Appendices
	1916			
N. MAROC	Oct 10		In Reserve Billets auc	
"	" 11		In Reserve Billets auc 2/Lt A.A. REDDING was presented with By Military Cross (ribbon)	
"	" 12		Moved to Reserve Billets Mazingarbe, taking over from 11th Bn Royal Lancaster auc	
MAZINGARBE	" 13		Moved into Front Line at LOOS, as right Batt: 14 BIS. SECTOR. Took over from 20th Middlesex On our left are 21st MIDDLESEX + on our right 19th Royal WELSH FUSILIERS. Quiet auc	
14 BIS	" 14		Slight Trench Mortar Activity auc	
	" 15		At 12.30 a.m the enemy blew a Mine at N.1.a.0.7 doing considerable damage to our Front Trench + causing several casualties to the Miners. No further action was taken by them. The remainder of the day was very quiet auc	
	" 16		We bombarded the enemy heavily with Trench Mortars during the day. M.G activity on both sides during the night auc.	
	" 17		Trench Mortar + Artillery Activity during the morning. Some enemy shelling during the night auc. 2/Lt. H WILLIAMS evacuated Gassed through mine on 15/10/16 auc	
"	" 18		Quiet auc 2/LT A.N ROCKER wounded while on Patrol auc	
	" 19		Quiet Some R.G + T.M activity. No enemy retaliation auc	

T2134. Wt. W708—776. 50000. 4/15. Sir J. C. & S.

Sheet III   WAR DIARY or INTELLIGENCE SUMMARY   12th Bn Suffolk Regt   Army Form C. 2118.

(Erase heading not required.)

Place	Date	Hour	Summary of Events and Information	Remarks and references to Appendices
	1916			
14 BIS	Oct 20		We find R.E. & T.M. drawing practically no fire from the enemy	A.W.C
	" 21		Relieved by 20th MIDDX. Moved in Support & Reserve	A.W.C
	" 22		Two Companys in Support & two in Reserve at MAZINGARBE	A.W.C
MAZINGARBE	" 23		" " " " " " " " " " "	A.W.C
	" 24		" " " " " " " " " " "	A.W.C
	" 25		" " " " " " " " " " "	A.W.C
	" 26		" " " " " " " " " " "	A.W.C
	" 27		Relieved by 1st ROYAL FUSILIERS in VILLAGE LINE & 8th BUFFS in MAZINGARBE. The Batt. moved to LES BREBIS	A.W.C
LES BREBIS	" 28		In LES BREBIS	A.W.C
BRUAY	" 29		The Batt. marched to BRUAY, starting at 4.45 a.m	A.W.C
CHELERS	" 30		The Batt. marched to CHELERS starting at 8.25 a.m	A.W.C
	" 31		In Billets in CHELERS	A.W.C

T. Rawley-Wilmot
Lt Col

CONFIDENTIAL

WAR DIARY

1st (G) Bn SUFFOLK REGT

From 1/11/16 To 30/11/16

Volume VI

Original Copy

9268

Only additional information regarding "wanting to complete" is to be entered on this side.

For information of the A.G.'s Office at the Base.

Officers and men who have become casuals, been transferred or joined since last report.

Place _____ Date _____

Regtl. Number	Rank	Name	Corps		Nature of casualty, or name of unit from or to which transferred	Date of being struck off or coming on the ration return	Remarks*
				Lost			

* State whether absence is of a permanent or temporary nature, adding, in the case of casuals from wounds or disease, any available information for communication to the relatives.

To be made up to and for Sunday in each week.

FIELD RETURN.

No. of Report_____   Army Form B. 213.

(To be furnished by all arms, services, and departments (except A.S.C. units) to the A. G.'s Office at the Base in accordance with Field Service Regulations, Part II.)

RETURN showing numbers (a) Effective strength of Unit.
                        (b) Rationed by Unit.   _____at_____ Date.

Detail	Personnel			Animals.							Guns, carriages, and limbers and transport vehicles											Remarks
				Horses			Mules							Horsed		Mechanical						
	Officers	Other ranks	Natives	Riding	Draught	Heavy Draught	Pack	Large	Small	Camels	Oxen	Guns, carriages and limbers, showing description	Ammunition wagons and limbers	Machine guns	Aircraft, showing description	4 wheeled	2 wheeled	Motor Cars.	Tractors	Lorries, showing description	Trucks, showing description	Trailers	Motor Bicycles	Bicycles	
Effective Strength of Unit																									
Details, *by Arms* attached to unit as in War Establishment:—																									
Total																									
War Establishment																									
Wanting to complete (Detail of Personnel and Horses below)																									
Surplus																									
*Attached (not to include the details shown above)																									
Civilians :— Employed with the Unit																									
Accompanying the Unit																									
Total Rationed...																									

* In the case of field ambulances, hospitals or depots, the number of patients are to be included here, the names being shown in A. F. A. 36.

_____Signature of Commander.

_____Date of Despatch.

WAR DIARY
INTELLIGENCE SUMMARY

Army Form C. 2118.

1st/5th B. Suffolks

Place	Date	Hour	Summary of Events and Information	Remarks and references to Appendices
			1916	
CHELERS	Mar 1		9th Batt in billets in CHELERS. keeping LENS II [illeg]	OMC
	2		9th Batt marched to billets in REBREUVIETTE	OMC
REBREUVIETTE	3		Jn billets in REBREUVIETTE	OMC
BARLY	4		9th Batt marched to billets in BARLY	OMC
BERNEVIL	5		Marched to billets in BERNEVIL	OMC
"	6		Jn billets in BERNEVIL	OMC
"	7		" " " "	OMC
"	8		" " " "	OMC
"	9		" " " "	OMC
"	10		" " " "	OMC
"	11		" " " "	OMC
"	12		" " " "	OMC
"	13		" " " "	OMC
"	14		Jn billets in BERNEVIL. 3 officers 2/Lt H.E.A. REYNOLDS, 2/Lt R. TRICKER	
"	15		2/Lt P.W. IVENS from 3rd Suffolks OMC	
VILLERS L'HOPITAL	" 15		9th Bge moved to billets in VILLERS L'HOPITAL	OMC

Sheet II   WAR DIARY or INTELLIGENCE SUMMARY.   12th B. Suffolk Regt.   Army Form C. 2118.

(Erase heading not required.)

Place	Date	Hour	Summary of Events and Information	Remarks and references to Appendices
	Nov 1916			
VILLERS L'HÔPITAL	16		In Billets in VILLERS L'HÔPITAL	AWC
BOUQUEMAISON	17		Moved to Billets in BOUQUEMAISON	AWC
SUS ST LEGER	18		Moved to Billets in SUS ST LEGER	AWC
"	19		In Billets in SUS ST LEGER	AWC
"	20		" " " " "	AWC
"	21		" " " " "	AWC
DOULLENS	22		The Batt moved to billets in DOULLENS	AWC
BERTEAUCOURT	23		The Batt moved to billets in BERTEAUCOURT	AWC
PONT-REMY	24		The Batt moved to billets in PONT-REMY	AWC
"	25		In billets in PONT-REMY	AWC
MOUFLERS	26		The Batt moved to billets in MOUFLERS	AWC
"	27		In billets in MOUFLERS	AWC
"	28		" " " "	AWC
"	29		" " " "	AWC
"	30		" " " "	AWC

T. Hawley Lockwith
Lt Col.
Comdg 12 B Suffolk Regt.

WAR DIARY or INTELLIGENCE SUMMARY

Sheet 1 — 12th H.L.I. Support Regt.
Army Form C. 2118.

Place	Date	Hour	Summary of Events and Information	Remarks and references to Appendices
MOUFLERS Dec?	1916 1		In billets at MOUFLERS. Map LENS 11 1/100,000	
"	2		" " " "	amc
"	3		" " " "	amc
"	4		" " " "	amc
"	5–10		" " " "	amc
Camp 12½ SAILLY LE SEC	11		Bn moved to SAILLY LE SEC via LONGPRÉ Stn and Rail = DERNANCOURT. Arrived by noon. Drew out MAP AMIENS 1/100,000 9/15	
"	12		In billets at SAILLY LE SEC	amc
"	13–25		In billets at SAILLY LE SEC	amc
"	26		Bttn moved to Camp 17. Map of ALBERT G8/4/9/9 1/10,000	amc
Camp 17 SUZANNE	28		In billets at Camp 17. Bergeaux in Reserve	amc
"	29		" " " "	amc
"	30		" " " "	amc
"	31		M.B. Provided Brigadier & Kent one gun 14th Argyll Sutherland Highlanders at C1/C6/? Map BOUCHEVESNES 1/10,000. Th...?	/21

Vol 7

Confidential

WAR DIARY

12th & 2nd SUFFOLK REGT.

From 1/1/17
to 31/1/17

(Volume 8)

Original

Vol 8

(B 9951) Wt. W15519/M149. 1/16. 1,000,000. J. F. & Co., Ltd. Forms/B 213/7.

[P.T.O.

Perforated Sheet giving detail of personnel and horses wanting to complete, shown on Army Form B. 213.

Number of Report _____

Remarks:— _____

Signature of Commander. _____

Unit. _____

Formation to which attached. _____

Date of Despatch. _____

	CAVALRY	R.A.	R.E.	INFANTRY	R.A.M.C.	A.O.C.	A.V.C.	
Drivers {								} Steam
								Lorry
								Car
								A.S.C.
								R.E.
								R.A.
Detail of Wanting to Complete {								} Gunners
								Smith Gunners
								Range Takers
								Serjeants
								Corporals
								Farriers
								Shoeing, or Shoeing and Carriage Smiths
								Cold Shoers
								R.A. Wheelers
								H. T.
								M. T.
								Saddlers or Harness Makers
								Blacksmiths
								Bricklayers and Masons
								Carpenters and Joiners
								Fitters & Turners (R. E.) Wood
								Iron
								R. A. Fitters
								Wireless
								Plumbers
								Ordinary Electricians
								W. T.
								Signalmen
								Loco. Engine Drivers
								Field
								Air Line Men
								Permanent Line Men
								Operators, Telegraph
								Cablemen
								Brigade Section Pioneers
								General-Duty Pioneers
								Signallers
								Instrument Repairers
								Motor Cyclists
								Motor Cyclist Artificers
								Telephonists
								Clerks
								Machine Gunners
								Fitters Armament Artificers
								Range Finders
								Armourers
								Storemen
								Privates
W.O.'s and N.C.O.'s (by ranks) not included in trade columns								
TOTAL to agree with wanting to complete								
Horses {								} Officers
								Other Ranks
								Riding
								Draught
								Heavy Draught
								Pack

Sheet I   **WAR DIARY** or **INTELLIGENCE SUMMARY**   12th Bn Suffolk Regt.   Army Form C. 2118.

(Erase heading not required.)

Place	Date	Hour	Summary of Events and Information	Remarks and references to Appendices
	Jan 1917			
BOUCHAVESNES	1st		In Front Line. 20th Middlesex on left. French on right. Map Ref: 62°N.W. C.9.d a.m.c	
"	2		Quiet until 10.15 pm when heavy hostile barrage on B.H.Q, Front & Support Line. Our Artillery silenced him at 11.15 pm a.m.c	
"	3		Quiet a.m.c	
"	4		Usual shelling on both sides. 2/Lt W.H. SLATER wounded a.m.c	
Camp 33	5		Relieved by 13th Yorkshire Regt. on night of 4/5th Jan. The Batt moved into Reserve at Camp 33 a.m.c	
"	6		In Reserve a.m.c	
"	7		" " a.m.c	
"	8		" " Relieved by 19th R.W.F. The Bn moved to Camp 17 at	
Camp 17			SUZANNE as Brigade in Reserve a.m.c	
"	9		In Camp 17. 2/Lt AGDAVEY, 2/Lt L.H. KNOWLES, 2/Lt R.T. ROBINS reported for duty a.m.c	
"	10		" " " a.m.c	
"	11		" " " a.m.c	
"	12		Took on Front Line at RANCOURT from 14th Argyll Sutherland Highlanders a.m.c	
RANCOURT	13		In Front Line. 20th Middx on left. 119th Brigade on right a.m.c	

Sheet II — 13th Suffolk Regt.

WAR DIARY
or
INTELLIGENCE SUMMARY.
(Erase heading not required.)

Instructions regarding War Diaries and Intelligence Summaries are contained in F. S. Regs., Part II. and the Staff Manual respectively. Title pages will be prepared in manuscript.

Army Form C. 2118.

Place	Date	Hour	Summary of Events and Information	Remarks and references to Appendices
	Jan 1917			
RANCOURT	14		In Front Line. Quiet. A.M.C	
"	15		" " Normal. A.M.C	
"	16		" " Relieved by 13th Bn Yorkshire Regt. Moved into Support. A.M.C	
"	17		In Support A.M.C	
"	18		" " A.M.C	
"	19		" " A.M.C	
"	20		" " Took over Front line from 13th Bn Yorkshire Regt. 20th Middx on left. East Surreys 10th Brigade on right. Quiet. A.M.C	
"	21		Heavy hostile shelling. A.M.C	
"	22		Usual shelling on both sides. Relieved by 19th R.W.F. & moved to Camp 17 as Brigade in Reserve. A.M.C	
Camp 17	23		In Camp 17. A.M.C	
"	24		" " A.M.C	
Camp 13.) CHIPILLY	25		Moved to Camp 13. CHIPILLY (ALBERT MAP) Division in Reserve. A.M.C	
"	26		In Camp 13. A.M.C	
"	27		Moved to Camp at BELAIR Railhead K19. ALBERT map. A.M.C	

T2134. Wt. W708—776. 500000. 4/15. Sir J. C. & S.

Sheet III — WAR DIARY or INTELLIGENCE SUMMARY — 12th Suffolk Regt. — Army Form C. 2118.

Place	Date	Hour	Summary of Events and Information	Remarks and references to Appendices
	Jan 1917			
BELAIR	28		At Belair a.m.c	
"	29		" " a.m.c	
"	30		" " a.m.c	
"	31		" " a.m.c	

Lennie Lloyd Major
Comdg 12th Suffolk Regt.

To be made up to and for Sunday in each week.

No. of Report _____

FIELD RETURN.

Army Form B. 213.

(To be furnished by all arms, services, and departments (except A.S.C. units) to the A. G.'s Office at the Base in accordance with Field Service Regulations, Part II.)

RETURN showing numbers (a) Effective strength of Unit.
                         (b) Rationed by Unit.
_____ at _____ _____ Date.

DETAIL	Personnel			Animals.								Guns, carriages, and limbers and transport vehicles												REMARKS
				Horses			Mules										Horsed				Mechanical				
	Officers	Other ranks	Natives	Riding	Draught	Heavy Draught	Pack	Large	Small	Camels	Oxen	Guns, carriages and limbers, showing description	Ammunition wagons and limbers	Machine guns	Aircraft, showing description	4 wheeled	2 wheeled	Motor Cars.	Tractors	Lorries, showing description	Trucks, showing description	Trailers	Motor Bicycles	Bicycles	
Effective Strength of Unit																									
Details, *by Arms* attached to unit as in War Establishment :—																									
Total																										
War Establishment																										
Wanting to complete (Detail of Personnel and Horses below)																										
Surplus																										
*Attached (not to include the details shown above)																										
Civilians :— Employed with the Unit Accompanying the Unit																										
TOTAL RATIONED...																										

* In the case of field ambulances, hospitals or depots, the number of patients are to be included here, the names being shown in A. F. A. 36.

_____ Signature of Commander.

_____ Date of Despatch.

For information of the A.G.'s Office at the Base.

Officers and men who have become casuals, been transferred or joined since last report.

Place.......................... Date..........................

Regtl. Number	Rank	Name	Corps	Nature of casualty, or name of unit from or to which transferred	Date of being struck off or coming on the ration return	Remarks*

* State whether absence is of a permanent or temporary nature, adding, in the case of casuals from wounds or disease, any available information for communication to the relatives.

WAR DIARY
12th B^n SUFFOLK REG^T

From Feb 1st To. Feb 28th

Confidential Original

Sheet I   WAR DIARY   12th B. Suffolk Regt   Army Form C. 2118.
or
INTELLIGENCE SUMMARY.
(Erase heading not required.)

Place	Date	Hour	Summary of Events and Information	Remarks and references to Appendices
	February			
BEL AIR Camp.	1st		In Huts in Bel Air Camp. G.H.Q. reserve a.m.c.	
	2		" " " " " " " a.m.c	
	3		" " " " " " " a.m.c	
	4		" " " " " " " a.m.c	
	5		" " " " " " " a.m.c	
	6		" " " " " " " a.m.c	
	7		" " " " " " " a.m.c	
	8		" " " " " " " a.m.c	
	9		" " " " " " " a.m.c	
Camp 111	10		" " " " " " moved to Camp 111 L.2.b. ALBERT Sheet a.m.c	
"	11		In Huts at Camp 111 a.m.c	
	12		" " " " a.m.c	
	13		" " " " a.m.c	
	14		" " " " a.m.c LT. SCHIFF, LT. J. LEE. 2/Lt. SMITH HALLSMITH, LOWRY MILLER reported for duty a.m.c	
	15		" " " " a.m.c	
	16		" " " " a.m.c	

WAR DIARY
INTELLIGENCE SUMMARY

Sqn I 12th F.S. Squadron R.F.C.

Army Form C. 2118.

Place	Date	Hour	Summary of Events and Information	Remarks and references to Appendices
Camp III	1915 Aug			
	17		2/Lt W. Corpin ¾/L A/C. Barrows M.C. reported for duty.	OMC
"	18			OMC
"	19			OMC
"	20			OMC
"	21			OMC
"	22		Recce ½ coy of MAUREPAS RAVINE a ferme BTT	OMC
MAUREPAS	23		Patrol recco.	OMC
"	24		Patrol Sud fut BANCOURT from 13th Division left. OMC 2nd Middlesex on right 50th Middlesex on left one	
BANCOURT	25		At Grand fere. Quiet morning. Heavy enemy shelling at 8.30pm which was silenced by our fire. OMC	
	26		The enemy continued shelling throughout the morning until 2am. Very heavy shelling on our left at 6pm. OMC	
	27		Fairly Quiet. OMC	
	28		10am. 2/Lt Middleton made a raid on an enemy front. At 5.25am we discovered enemy carrying out XIV Corps on the left who attacked at the same time, responding with XIV Corps on the left who attacked at the same time. The enemy opened a heavy artillery fire in front of our line during the	

Sheet III — WAR DIARY or INTELLIGENCE SUMMARY — 12th Bn Suffolk Regt — Army Form C. 2118.

Place	Date	Hour	Summary of Events and Information	Remarks and references to Appendices
			damage. Relieved by 13th Yorks in the evening & marched back to Reserve at MAUREPAS. Gas shells fell by COMBLES Road as the Batt marched back. One Left Coy H.Q shelled with gas shells during evening. B.	

T. Dudley-Woodroffe Lt Col
Comdg 12th Bn Suffolk Regt

WAR DIARY
or
INTELLIGENCE SUMMARY.

Army Form C. 2118.

1/5th Suffolk Regt

Place	Date	Hour	Summary of Events and Information	Remarks and references to Appendices
Camp 165 MAYREFAS	March 1917 1		In the of Camp 165 Bn in Reserve	OMC
	2		" " " " "	OMC
	3		" " " " "	OMC
RANCOURT	4		Took over trenches from 13th Yorkshire Regt	
			Relief completed 10 p.m. 30" bale on left. 2nd bn Yorks on right	
			Heavy shelling on our right all night	OMC
RANCOURT	5		Enemy artillery very active all day. 3/s E A BARDEN wounded	OMC
	6		Our Artillery active. All enemy fires ordered OMC	
	6		Quiet, Relieved by 2nd Scottish Rifles, 7/muskin + Pte BONNETT (B310528)	
			ALBERT T Shot 4.9.9.0	OMC
Lt BONNETT	8		Marched to Camp 17	OMC
CAMP 17	9		In billets at Camp 17	OMC
"	10		"	OMC
"	11		"	OMC
"	12		"	OMC
"	13		"	OMC

AH 10

Sheet II **WAR DIARY** 12th Bn Suffolk Regt
or
INTELLIGENCE SUMMARY
(Erase heading not required.)

Army Form C. 2118.

Place	Date	Hour	Summary of Events and Information	Remarks and references to Appendices
Camp 17	14		In Huts at Camp 17. AWC	
"	15		Moved to Batt in Support at P.C. MERTON H.6.a.8.6 ALBERT Sheet. Took over from 17th Welsh. AWC	
P.C. MERTON	16		In Support Quiet AWC	
"	17		In Support. Quiet 2 Platoons were attached to 21st Middlesex Regt at 7 pm as they advanced. Enemy retired from their line, still moving forward AWC	
"	18		In Support Withdrew the 2 Platoons from 21st Middlesex. They were relieved by 20th Middlesex who moved up at 8.30 am. Sent 1 Company (A) to 13th Yorkshires. Enemy has retired from the line on whole front AWC	
PERONNE	19		CO and Capt S. .... PERONNE AWC Moved up to a position just NW of PERONNE with 1 Company (B) as Outpost Coy at THREE TUBS WOOD J.19.C. 48th Division on Right 20th Middx on left. AWC	
"	20		Outpost Coy withdrawn. The position being taken over by 48th Division. The Batt remained in position NW of PERONNE AWC	
Mt ST QUINTON	21		Orders to move into Mt ST QUINTON to relieve the 20th MIDDLESEX. Took over from them at 7 am. AWC	

Sheet III   **WAR DIARY**   12ᵗʰ Bn Suffolk Regt.   Army Form C. 2118.

Instructions regarding War Diaries and Intelligence Summaries are contained in F. S. Regs., Part II. and the Staff Manual respectively. Title pages will be prepared in manuscript.

or

INTELLIGENCE SUMMARY.

(Erase heading not required.)

Place	Date	Hour	Summary of Events and Information	Remarks and references to Appendices
	March			
Mᵗ Sᵗ QUINTON	22		Two Companies moved up in Support to 20ᵗʰ MIDDLESEX who were holding the line and finding Outposts A.W.C.	
"	23		Generally clearing up & remaking roads in Mᵗ Sᵗ QUINTON A.W.C	
"	24		In Mᵗ Sᵗ QUINTON A.W.C	
CAMP at	25		Moved to Camp at I.8.C A.W.C Ref PERONNE. MAP	
I.8.G.	26		The Batt. remaking roads from HAUT ALLAINES to MOISLAIN A.W.C	
"	27		" " " " 2/LT F.C. SMITH reported for duty A.W.C	
"	28		" " " " 2/LᵀI. GRIFFITHS reported for duty A.W.C	
"	29		" " " " A.W.C	
"	30		" " " " A.W.C	
"	31		" " " " A.W.C	

T. Lawley Wilworth
Lt Col
Comdg 12ᵗʰ Suffolk Regt.

T2134. Wt. W708—776. 500000. 4/15. Sir J. C. & S.

WAR DIARY
of
1st Bn SUFFOLK REGT

From April 1st 1917
To April 30th 1917

Volume XI
(Original Copy)

(5817) Wt. W4778/M669 700,000 8/16 D.D. & L., Ltd. (E. 272) Forms/b.213/8.

Only additional information regarding wanting to complete is to be entered on this side.

[P.T.O.]

Date of Despatch _____

Formation to which attached _____

Unit _____

Signature of Commander _____

Remarks :—

Perforated Sheet giving detail of personnel and horses wanting to complete, shown on Army Form B. 213.

No. of Report _____

		CAVALRY	R.A.	R.E.	INFANTRY	R.A.M.C.	A.O.C.	A.V.C.		
Detail of Wanting to Complete.										
Drivers	R.A.									
	R.E.									
	A.S.C.									
	Car									
	Lorry									
	Steam									
	Gunners									
	Smith Gunners									
	Range Takers									
	Serjeants									
	Corporals									
	Shoeing, or Shoeing and Carriage Smiths									
	Farriers									
	Cold Shoers									
	R.A.									
	H.T.	Wheelers								
	M.T.									
	Saddlers or Harness Makers									
	Blacksmiths									
	Bricklayers and Masons									
	Carpenters and Joiners									
	Wood	Fitters & Turners (R.E.)								
	Iron									
	R.A.	Fitters								
	Wireless									
	Plumbers									
	Ordinary	Electricians								
	W.T.									
	Signalmen									
	Loco.	Engine Drivers								
	Field									
	Air Line Men									
	Permanent Line Men									
	Operators, Telegraph									
	Cablemen									
	Brigade Section Pioneers									
	General-duty Pioneers									
	Signallers									
	Instrument Repairers									
	Motor Cyclists									
	Motor Cyclist Artificers									
	Telephonists									
	Clerks									
	Machine Gunners									
	Range Finders									
	Fitters	Armament Artificers								
	Armourers									
	Storemen									
	Privates									
W.O.'s and N.C.O.'s (by ranks) not included in trade columns										
TOTAL to agree with wanting to complete.	Officers									
	Other Ranks									
Horses	Riding									
	Draught									
	Heavy Draught									
	Pack									

To be made up to and for Sunday in each week

No. of Report _____   **FIELD RETURN.**   Army Form B. 213.

(To be furnished by all arms, services, and departments (except A.S.C. units) to the A.G.'s Office at the Base in accordance with Field Service Regulations, Part II.)

RETURN showing numbers (a) Effective strength of Unit.
(b) Rationed by Unit. _____ at _____ _____ Date.

DETAIL	Personnel			Animals								Guns, carriages, and limbers and transport vehicles												REMARKS
				Horses				Mules				Guns, carriages and limbers, showing description	Ammunition wagons and limbers	Machine guns	Aircraft, showing description	Horsed		Mechanical				Motor Bicycles	Bicycles	
	Officers	Other ranks	Natives	Riding	Draught	Heavy Draught	Pack	Large	Small	Camels	Oxen					4 Wheeled	2 Wheeled	Motor Cars	Tractors	Lorries, showing description	Trucks showing description	Trailers			
Effective Strength of Unit.....																									
Details *by Arms* attached to unit as in War Establishment:—																									
Total																									
War Establishment																									
Wanting to complete (Detail of Personnel and Horses below)																									
Surplus																									
*Attached (not to include the details shown above)...........																									
Civilians:— Employed with the Unit																									
Accompanying the Unit																									
Total Rationed																									

* In the case of field ambulances, hospitals or depots, the number of patients are to be included here, the names being shown in A. F. A. 36.

_____ Signature of Commander.   _____ Date of Despatch.

Sheet I WAR DIARY 12th Bn Suffolk Regt. Army Form C. 2118
or
INTELLIGENCE SUMMARY.
(Erase heading not required.)

Place	Date	Hour	Summary of Events and Information	Remarks and references to Appendices
	April			
Mt ST QUINTON	1		In Camp at Mt ST QUINTON I.9.C.4.5.	aul
I.9.C.4.5	2		" " " "	aul
Sheet 62C NW	3		" " " "	aul
	4		" " " "	aul
	5		" " " "	aul
FINS	6		Moved up as Batt in Brigade Support at FINS V.12.6.8.2 Sheet 57C SE	
V.12.6.8.2			2 Company's at FINS and 2 Company at DESART WOOD.	aul
Sheet 57C SE	7		In FINS as above Batt in Brigade Support.	aul
	8		" " " " " " "	aul
	9		" " " " " " " 3 Coys. in DESART WOOD	aul
	10		" " " " " " "	aul
DESART WOOD	11		In DESART WOOD as Bn. in Brigade Support.	aul
W.1.C.2.2	12		" " " " " " "	aul
Sheet 57C SE	13		" " " " " " "	aul
QUEENS CROSS	14		At Queens Cross. Q.28.d.3-2. as Right Bn. in Line	aul Lt J. LEE Wounded aul
Q.28.d.3-2	15		" " " " " " "	aul
Sheet 57C SE				

Sheet 2.

WAR DIARY
or
INTELLIGENCE SUMMARY

Army Form C. 2118.

12th Bn. Suffolk Regt.

Place	Date	Hour	Summary of Events and Information	Remarks and references to Appendices
	April			
	16		ot QUEENS CROSS @ 28d3-2. 08 Right Coy in huts.	
	17		" " " " " " " " "	
ETRICOURT	18		ot ETRICOURT. Bdc in Reserve	
Q28 8-3	19		" " " " " "	
Short 57cSE	20		" " " " " "	
	21		" " " " " "	
	22		" " " " " "	
	23		" " " " " "	
	24		Moved up to DES ART WOOD to support 120th Bn. not required & returned to EQUANCOURT in evening	
	25		ot EQUANCOURT. Moved to QUEENS CROSS in line of resistance.	
QUEENS CROSS	26		ot QUEENS CROSS 2 Coys in @ 25C & 2 Coys in @ 24a in support to front line.	
	27		" " " " " " " " "	
	28		" " " " " " " " "	
	29		" " " " " " " " " Army	
	30		Relieved the 19th Royal Welsh Fusiliers in front line at Prevailing Cuts Ridges	

WAR DIARY or INTELLIGENCE SUMMARY

Sheet 3   12th Bn Suffolk Regt   Army Form C. 2118.

(Erase heading not required.)

Place	Date	Hour	Summary of Events and Information	Remarks and references to Appendices
			of the Divisional front. The 119th Brigade on our Right, 13th Yorkshire Regt on our left. AWC	

T. Pardey Coot and h
Lt Col
30/4/17

For information of the A.G.'s Office at the base.

Officers and men who have become casuals, been transferred or joined since last report.

Place _____   Date _____

Regtl. Number	Rank	Name	Corps	Nature of casualty, or name of unit from or to which transferred	Date of being struck off or coming on the ration return	Remarks*

*State whether absence is of a permanent or temporary nature, adding, in the case of casuals from wounds or disease, any available information for communication to the relatives.

[P.T.O.

To be made up to and for Saturday in each week

No. of Report _____

FIELD RETURN.

Army Form B 213

(To be furnished by all arms, services, and departments (except A.S.C. units) to the A.G.'s Office at the Base in accordance with Field Service Regulations, Part II.)

RETURN showing numbers (a) Effective strength of Unit.
(b) Rationed by Unit.

_____ at _____ _____ Date.

DETAIL	Personnel			Animals						Guns and transport vehicles.													REMARKS
				Horses				Mules						Horsed		Mechanical							
	Officers	Other ranks	Natives	Riding	Draught	Heavy Draught	Pack	Large	Small	Guns, showing description	Ammunition wagons	Machine guns	Aircraft, showing description	4 Wheeled	2 Wheeled	Motor Cars	Tractors	Lorries, showing description	Trucks, showing description	Trailers	Motor Bicycles	Bicycles	Motor Ambulances	
Effective Strength of Unit......																								
Details *by Arms* attached to unit as in War Establishment :—																								
Total																								
War Establishment																								
Wanting to complete (Detail of Personnel and Horses below)																								
Surplus																								
*Attached (not to include the details shown above)..........																								
Civilians :— Employed with the Unit																								
Accompanying the Unit																								
TOTAL RATIONED......																								

* In the case of field ambulances, hospitals or depots, the number of patients are to be included here, the names being shown in A.F.A. 36.

_____ Signature of Commander. _____ Date of Despatch.

Demands made on this sheet should consist of personnel required from the Base only, and should not include any demands for personnel which can be completed by promotions or appointments within the unit.

Perforated Sheet giving detail of personnel and horses wanting to complete, shown on Army Form B. 213.

No. of Report _____

Detail of Wanting to Complete.	Drivers						Gunners	Swift. Gunners	Range-Takers	Farriers		Shoeing, or Shoeing and Carriage Smiths	Cold Shoers	Wheelers			Saddlers or Harness Makers	Blacksmiths	Bricklayers and Masons	Carpenters and Joiners	Fitters & Turners (R.E.)		Fitters		Plumbers	Electricians		W.T.	Signalmen	Engine Drivers		Air Line Men	Permanent Line Men	Operators, Telegraph	Cablemen	Brigade Section Pioneers	General-duty Pioneers	Signallers	Instrument Repairers	Motor Cyclist	Motor Cyclist Artificers	Telephonists	Clerks	Machine Gunners	Fitters	Range Finders	Armament Artificers		Armourers	Storemen	Privates	W.O's. and N.C.O's. (by ranks) not included in trade columns					TOTAL to agree with wanting to complete		Horses			
	R.A.	R.E.	A.S.C.	Car	Lorry	Steam				Serjeants	Corporals			R.A.	H.T.	M.T.					Wood	Iron	R.A.	Wireless		Ordinary				Loco.	Field																										Officers	Other Ranks	Riding	Draught	Heavy Draught	Park
CAVALRY																																																												
R.A.																																																												
R.E.																																																												
INFANTRY																																																												
R.A.M.C.																																																												
A.O.C.																																																												
A.V.C.																																																												

Remarks :—

_____ Signature of Commander.

_____ Unit,

_____ Formation to which attached.

_____ Date of Despatch.

D. D. & L. London, E.C.
(7422) Wt. W14775/M1553 1,000,000 2/17 (E934) Forms B213/8

[P.T.O.

FIELD RETURN

For information of the A.G.'s Office at the base.

Officers and men who have become casuals, been transferred or joined since last report.

Place _____   Date _____

Regtl. Number	Rank	Name	Corps	Nature of casualty, or name of unit from or to which transferred	Date of being struck off or coming on the ration return	Remarks*

*State whether absence is of a permanent or temporary nature, adding, in the case of casuals from wounds or disease, any available information for communication to the relatives.

July 1.
12th Batt Suffolk Regt

WAR DIARY
INTELLIGENCE SUMMARY

Army Form C. 2118.

Place	Date	Hour	Summary of Events and Information	Remarks and references to Appendices
Thes VILLERS Rovich R13 Map 57c SE	May 1		A front line relief 12" S W B m the night. 13" Yorkshire Regt on left. 3rd Yorks were relieved by 14th H.L.I. Our Batt HQ and R in c.o.o. map 57C SE 20.000	
	2		Heavy trench shelling from midnight to dawn. The shirt on our left were relieved on night of 1/2" by 14th H.L.I. At night we observed an new trench running East + Timber with slight casualties. Our line is now approximately R15.a.0.4 - R15.a.0.0. - R15.c.0.6. Map	
	3		B.9 11. Total Casualties 20 OWG Quiet day. Some slight shelling of night. OWG	
	4		As opened a heavy on the enemy line at 11 am but did not attack even if it was replied vigorously but did no material damage. Remainder of the day very quiet except for our own guns.	
	5		Casualties NIL OWG Quiet morning. Our artillery continued very active, the enemy were scarcely shelling during the afternoon. At 11 pm in conjunction with 119th Brigade + 8th Division we carried out a raid on the enemy line B in the second	

Sheet II
WAR DIARY or INTELLIGENCE SUMMARY.
12th Bn Suffolk
Army Form C. 2118.

(Erase heading not required.)

Place	Date	Hour	Summary of Events and Information	Remarks and references to Appendices
	May 5		of LA VACQUERIE. The artillery opened a heavy barrage at 11 p.m. & we advanced under cover of it. A & D Coys carried out the operation. Shortly after the start Capt A.V. CRUMP was wounded in the thigh & foot. D.Coy suffered heavily from Machine Gun fire & was also held up by uncut wire over which they were bombed. A.Coy gained their objective but discovered that they were only dummy trenches. A party of this Company under Sgt LOVELL became separated from the main body & continued on toward the Hindenburg Line. After fighting & capturing a German patrol they were unable to find their way back & continued down a Sunken road toward LA VACQUERIE. On this road they came on a German Sentry whom they made prisoner & made him show them the way back. Total prisoners 4. Total Casualties Capt A.V. CRUMP wounded. OR Killed OR Wounded OR Missing	AWC
	6		Quiet. The Batt was relieved by 21st MIDDLESEX at 12 m.n. & marched back to DESART WOOD MAP 57C SE	AWC
DESART WOOD	7		In reserve	AWC
"	8			AWC

| | | | WAR DIARY *Sheet III* *12th Bn Suffolk Regt* | Army Form C. 2118. |

Instructions regarding War Diaries and Intelligence Summaries are contained in F. S. Regs., Part II. and the Staff Manual respectively. Title pages will be prepared in manuscript.

WAR DIARY
or
INTELLIGENCE SUMMARY.
(*Erase heading not required.*)

Place	Date	Hour	Summary of Events and Information	Remarks and references to Appendices
MAP. 57CSE	May			
DESART WOOD	9.		In Reserve AWC	
	10		" " AWC	
	11		" " AWC	
	12		" " AWC	
HEUDECOURT	13		" " Moved to HEUDECOURT in billets AWC	
"	14		In rest billets at HEUDECOURT. Moved to Front Line in evening to our Right Sat Sector VILLERS GUISLAIN from 1st Bn ROYAL IRISH RIFLES. 20th Bn MIDDLESEX on our left. 1/5th LANCASHIRE FUSILIERS on the ~~right~~ AWC	
VILLERS GUISLAIN	15		In Front Line. Quiet AWC	
	16		" " " Patrol were fired on from LES TRANCHÉES Casualties 3 O.R. AWC	
	17		Quiet day AWC	
	18		" " " AWC 5th Lancers relieved the Batt on our right AWC	
	19.		Quiet generally. Aeroplane activity on both Sides. Our patrols inflicted losses on the enemy. Our Casualties 3 O.R. wounded. 2/Lt A.N. RUCKER wounded, at duty AWC	
	20		Quiet day AWC	
	21		Very quiet. Our Aeroplanes more active than usual. Carried out a	

T.2134. Wt. W708—776. 500000. 4/15. Sir J. C. & S.

Sheet IV
WAR DIARY
15th Bn Suffolk Regt.
Army Form C. 2118.

Place	Date	Hour	Summary of Events and Information	Remarks and references to Appendices
VILLERS GUISLAIN			raid on Enemy at LES TRANCHEES about X 12 c and X 18 a. (map 57 C SE Edition 3A.) 3 parties under 2/Lt H. LEEMING 2/Lt L.C. WILLIAMS & Sgt GIPP. D.C.M left our trenches at 10 pm. The two latter parties entered the enemy system but did not meet any of the enemy at close enough quarters to secure any prisoner. 2/Lt H. LEEMING met a patrol before reaching the trench & after a short engagement captured a wounded prisoner belonging to 124th ERSATZ REGT. Another party under 2/Lt KNOWLES entered the enemy trench on western edge of HONNECOURT WOOD about X 11 d 1.9. Here again no prisoners were taken. It was an extremely dark night & nothing could be seen if more than about 1 foot away. It is believed several casualties were inflicted on the enemy. Our casualties 1. OR died of wounds 4. OR wounded.	
	22		All parties were back in our trenches by 1.30 am 22nd a AWL	
	22		Quiet, nothing to report. AWL	
	23		Quiet day. Relieved by 18th H.L.I & moved to DESSART WOOD arriving there at 4. AM 24th AWL	

			WAR DIARY	Army Form C. 2118.

Instructions regarding War Diaries and Intelligence Summaries are contained in F. S. Regs., Part II. and the Staff Manual respectively. Title pages will be prepared in manuscript.

WAR DIARY
or
INTELLIGENCE SUMMARY.
(Erase heading not required.)

Place	Date	Hour	Summary of Events and Information	Remarks and references to Appendices
	May 1917			
DESSART WOOD	24		Rest in DESSART WOOD aulc	
"	25		" " " " aulc	
"	26		" " " " Relieved 12th S.W.B. in Support to front line see	Appendix I
			Appendix I aulc	
GOUZEAUCOURT area	27.		No 27444 Sgt. G. JONES awarded MILITARY MEDAL see Appendix II	Appendix II
			Provided working parties for front line Batts: aulc	
"	28		In Support Quiet aulc	
"	29		" " Quiet aulc	
"	30		" " Quiet aulc	
"	31		" " Quiet Capt. A.H.M. JACKSON reported for duty from England aulc	
			Strength on May 1st 38. Off 880 OR	
			" " " 31st 39 " 781 "	
			Total Casualties during the month 1 Off: 140 OR.	
			" Reinforcements " " " 2 Off: 17 OR.	

T2134. Wt. W708—776. 500000. 4/15. Sir J. C. & S.

War Diary Appendix I

OPERATION ORDERS
BY
LIEUT COL. T. EARDLEY-WILMOT., D.S.O.
COMMANDING BATTALION SUFFOLK REGIMENT.

IN THE FIELD. 25th May, 1917.

1. The Battalion will relieve the 13th Bn. S.W.B. on night of 26/27th May, via QUEENS-CROSS.

2. Relief will be in following order:-
   "A", "B", "C", "D". Headquarters.
   On completion companies will be in following positions:-
   "A" Coy. SUNKEN ROAD.   Q.34.c.
   "B" "   SUNKEN ROAD.   Q.29.c.8.9.
   "C" "   Brown Line from Q.29.c. Eastward.
   "D" "   SUNKEN ROAD.   Q.30.b.
   H. Qrs.   Q.29.b.8.2.

3. Advance parties of 1 Officer and 1 N.C.O per coy. will report to Bn. H.Qrs. 13th S.W.B. at 6 p.m. 26th instant. They will take over accomodation and stores, including maps, and forward lists to Adjutant as soon as the companies arrive. They will meet their respective companies at QUEENS CROSS Cross Roads at 9 p.m.

4. Companies will march by platoons at 100 yards interval. No troops will pass QUEENS CROSS before 9.30 pm

5. Water tins will be carried. full on the inside. Water bottles will be filled.

6. One limber per company and one= Headquarters will report at 6 p.m. 26th instant, for carriage of Lewis Guns, etc. They will march in rear of first platoon of each company.

7. Completion of relief will be wired in usual code.

8. Officers kits will be collected at 6 p.m.
   (Signed) A.M. CROSS, Lieut & Adjt.

WAR DIARY Appendix II

40TH DIVISION.

LIST OF N.C.O'S AND MEN AWARDED THE MILITARY MEDAL.

No. 99207, Cpl.(A/Sgt.) ALBERT JENKINSON
Field Company, Royal Engineers.

During a raid on the enemy's positions on the night 5/6th May 1917, Sergt. JENKINSON showed great coolness and devotion to duty. Although heavily bombed and fired on by the enemy he did good work in placing charges and destroying buildings.

No. 45758, Private JAMES TRODDEN,
No. 29201, Private MICHAEL CULLEN,
both of Royal Welsh Fusiliers.

They led the way with great gallantry during a raid on the enemy's trenches on the night 5/6th May, 1917. They set an example which was greatly instrumental in the capture of the trench.

No. 23918, Lance-Corporal JAMES DAVID QUINN,
South Wales Borderers.

L/Cpl. QUINN was in charge of a section of the Battalion Signallers during a raid on the enemy's positions on the night 5/6th May, 1917. When all except one of his section had become casualties and he himself was wounded in the foot he continued to lay out his wire and established a signal station in a captured trench.

No. 26040, Sergeant JAMES DAVID HUGHES,
The Welsh Regiment.

Sergt. HUGHES showed great coolness and presence of mind in leading his party during a raid on the enemy's positions on the night 5/6th May, 1917. He was the last man to leave the enemy positions and ably conducted the withdrawal of his men.

No. 25992, Private JOHN HUMPHREY JONES,
The Welsh Regiment.

During a raid on the enemy's positions on the night 5/6th May 1917 Pte. JONES was Number 1 of his Platoon Lewis Gun Team. At a critical moment he brought his gun to bear on a party of the enemy at a range of about 30 or 40 yards. He behaved with great courage.

No. 23706, Private JOHN WOOD,
South Wales Borderers.

Pte. WOOD did extremely good work and displayed great courage during a raid on the enemy's positions on the night 5/6th May, 1917.

/over.

- 2 -

No. 25278 Lance-Corporal DENNIS PATRICK SULLIVAN,
The Welsh Regiment.

During a raid on the enemy's positions on the night 5/6th May 1917, L/Cpl. SULLIVAN led his section with much dash. He bombed and cleared an enemy trench in face of considerable opposition. He set a splendid example and showed great courage.

No. 25656, Private JAMES LEWIS,
The Welsh Regiment.

Pte. LEWIS acted as Company Runner during a raid on the enemy's positions on the night 5/6th May, 1917. His conduct throughout the operations was most praiseworthy; he continued taking messages through heavy rifle and machine gun fire until wounded in the right leg.

No. 27444, Sergeant GEORGE JONES,
Suffolk Regiment.

During the raid on the enemy's positions on the night 5/6th May 1917 every telephone wire to the Front Line was cut by the enemy's barrage. Sergt. JONES worked at repairing them under heavy shell fire. He displayed great gallantry.

Issued with Divisional Routine Orders, 26th May, 1917.

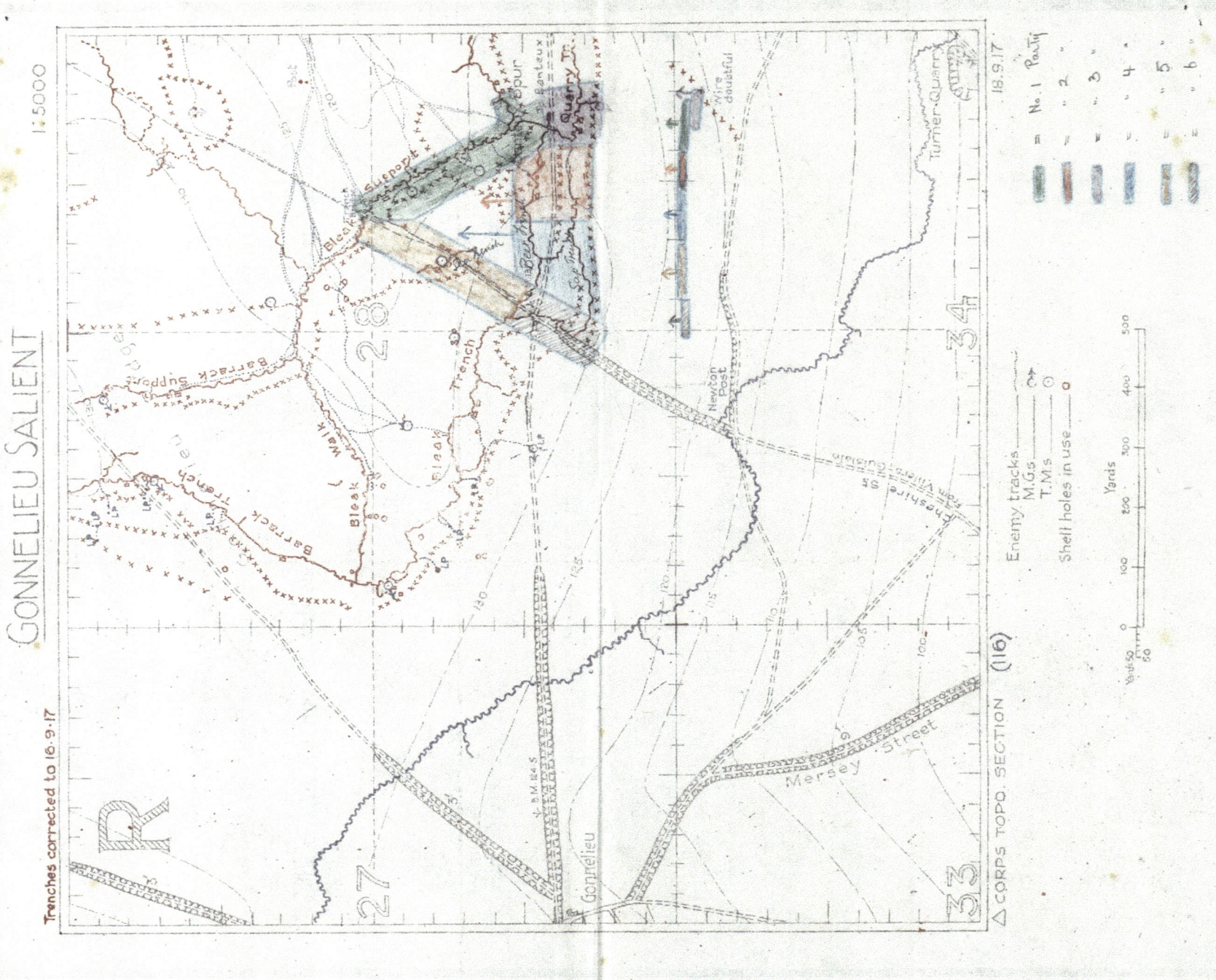

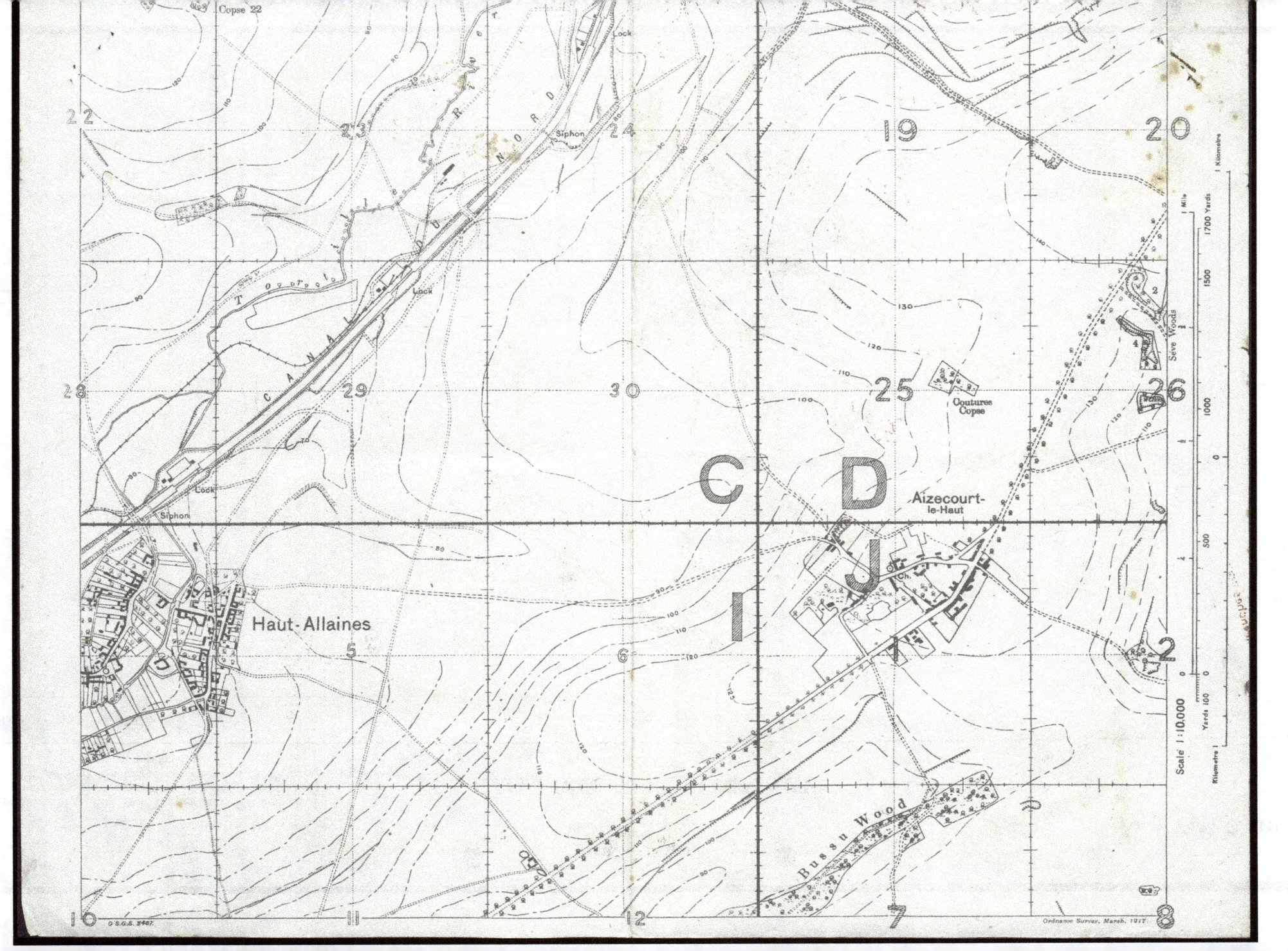

WAR DIARY or INTELLIGENCE SUMMARY

Army Form C. 2118

Sheet I

12th Bn Suffolk Regt

Place	Date	Hour	Summary of Events and Information	Remarks and references to Appendices
VILLERS FAUCON Sqd Q.36.c.5.5	June 1917 1		In support. Supplied working parties to front line during our forward push. Capt A.H.M. JACKSON wounded. OMG	AH/13
	2		In support. Work carried on as before. OMG	
	3		In support. Relieved by 8th WELSH Regt & remained in DESSART WOOD as part of Brigade in Reserve behind Front to 119 Brigade. OMG	
DESSART WOOD N.2.a. Map 57C SE	4		In Brigade in Reserve. OMG	
	5.6.7.		" " " " OMG OMG OMG	
	8		" " " " OMG	
			DCM awarded to 24668 Sgt J.F. LOVELL for gallant display during a raid on the enemy position of LA VACQUERIE on night of 5/6 April. OMG	
			DCM awarded to RSM C.W. MACEY in recognition of Meritorious Service. OMG	
			R.S.M. Macey died of wounds Aug 23rd	
			MAJOR J. LLOYD, Lt A.M. CROSS, the Rev W.CH. HURRELL mentioned in dispatches OMG	
	9		In Brigade in Reserve OMG	
	10		" " " " OMG	
	11		Moved to Front line in the GONNELIEU SECTOR from OMG	
			14th A+SH 20th MIDDLESEX on Left. 18th HLI on right (35th Div.) OMG	

1875 Wt. W593/826 1,000,000 4/15 J.B.C.&A. A.D.S. (Forms/C.2118.

WAR DIARY or **INTELLIGENCE SUMMARY** Sheet II 1st Suffolk

Army Form C. 2118

Instructions regarding War Diaries and Intelligence Summaries are contained in F. S. Regs., Part II. and the Staff Manual respectively. Title Pages will be prepared in manuscript.

(Erase heading not required.)

Place	Date	Hour	Summary of Events and Information	Remarks and references to Appendices
MAP 57C SE				
GONNELIEU	June 1917 12.		Quiet day. Very little Artillery fire. Dug second front line AMC	Map refs 57 C. SE 1/20,000
	13		" " Occasional fire by Artillery on both sides AMC	
	14		Quiet. Nothing to report AMC	
	15		Occasional Artillery fire, generally quiet AMC	
	16		5 OR killed by T.M. Gas shell otherwise quiet AMC	
	17		Occasional artillery fire AMC	
	18		Quiet. AMC	
	19		Quiet. Relieved by 13th YORKSHIRE REGT & moved to reserve with Bn H.Q. at W4.a.1.4. Map 57.C.SE AMC	
W4.a.1.4.	20		In Reserve AMC	
"	21		" " AMC	
W6.d.6.5.	22		" " moved A Coy to W.10.d.5.6. & Bn. H.Q. to W6.d.6.5. AMC	
"	23		" " AMC	
"	24		" " AMC	
"	25		" " AMC	
"	26		" " AMC	
"	27		" " Relieved by 17th WELSH REGT. & marched to camp at SOREL AMC	
SOREL	28		Brigade in Reserve AMC	
	29		" " AMC	
	30		" " AMC	

OPERATION ORDERS
BY
LIEUT COL. T. EARDLEY-WILMOT. D.S.O.,
COMMANDING BATTALION SUFFOLK REGIMENT.

IN-THE-FIELD.   2nd June, 1917.

1. The Battalion will be relieved by Units of 115th Brigade on night of 3/4th June, as under :-

   "A" Coy. Suffolks relieved by 17th Bn. Welch Regt.
   "B" Coy.   "   "   " 19th Bn. Royal Welch Fusirs
   "C" Coy.   "   "   " 19th Bn. Royal Welch Fusirs
   "D" Coy.   "   "   " 17th Bn. Welch Regt.
   H. Qrs.   "   "   " 19th Bn. Royal Welch Fusirs

   On relief companies will march to DESSART WOOD by platoons at 100 yards interval.

   Advance parties of 1 Officer and 1 N.C.O. per company and Headquarters will proceed to DESSART WOOD and take over stores and accommodation from 12th Bn. S.W.Bs. They will report to Headquarters, 12th Bn. S.W.Bs. at 3 p.m. 3rd instant.
   Companies will take over the same accommodation from S.W.Bs. as they vacated on 26th May.

   Trench Stores will be handed over and receipts forwarded to Orderly Room by 9 a.m. 4th June.

   Quartermaster will arrange for 1 Limber per company and 1 per Bn. Headquarters to report at Company and H.Q. ration dumps at 10 p.m. June 3rd, for carriage of Lewis Guns, etc.

   Completion of relief will be wired in usual code in present position and sent by runner on arrival at DESSART WOOD.

   Baths at FINS are allotted as under :-
           5th June, 1917.

   "A" Company 9 a.m. to 10 a.m.   1 p.m. to 2 p.m.
   "B"   "   10 a.m. to 11 a.m.   2 p.m. to 3 p.m.
   "C"   "   11 a.m. to 12 noon   3 p.m. to 4 p.m.
   "D"   "   12 noon to 1 p.m.   4 p.m. to 5 p.m.

All details will bathe with their companies. O.C. Companies will report by 7 p.m. 5th June, the number of men who have not bathed and the reason thereof.

Companies will clean up on 4th instant and all men must be clean and shaved by the evening of the 4th.

Companies will arrange for refitting on the 5th instant.

(Signed) A.K. CROSS,
Lieutenant,
& Adjutant,
Battalion Suffolk Regiment.

SECRET   Ref Map 5708E

OPERATION ORDERS
BY
LIEUT.COL.T.EARDLEY-WILMOT D.S.O.,
COMMANDING BATTALION SUFFOLK REGIMENT.
:-:-:-:-:-:-:-:-:-:-:-:-:-:-:-:-:-:-
IN THE FIELD.   June 18th 1917.

No.1. The Battalion will be relieved on night of 19/20 June by Yorkshire Regiment as under :-

SUFFOLKS   BY   YORKSHIRE
"A" Company & 1 Platoon "C" Coy.   BY   "B" Coy & 1Platoon "C" Coy
                                                in left Front.
"D"   "   & 1   "   "B" Coy   BY   "A" Coy & 1 Platoon "D" Coy
                                                in right Front.
3 Platoons "B" Coy   BY   3 Platoons "D" in Right
                                                Support.
3   "   "C" Coy   BY   3 Platoons "C" Coy in
                                                left Support.
Headquarters   BY   Headquarters.

No.2. On relief Companies will march by Platoons via R.E.Dump at R.26.C.5.0.to positions vacated by Yorkshire Regt :-

"A" Company will take over from "D" Company Yorks W.4.C.o.9.
"B"   "   "   "   "   "A"   "   "   X. 1.K.3.7.
"C"   "   "   "   "   "C"   "   "   W.6.D.6.2.
"D"   "   "   "   "   "B"   "   "   (Quentin Mill
                                                   (R.31.D.15.85.
Headquarters   "   "   "   Headquarters   "   W.4.A.1.2.
No.3. Advance parties of Suffolk Regt of 1 Officer & 1.N.C.O. per Company & Battalion Headquarters will report to Companies as in paragraph 2 at 4 p.m. 19th.
Advance parties of Yorkshire Regt will arrive at Battalion Headquarters at 3 P.M.

No.4. Guides will be found as under :-

BY SUFFOLK REGIMENT.

5 from "A" Company (1 per platoon)
3   " "B"   "   (1 "   "   )
3   " "C"   "   (1 "   "   )
3   " "D"   "   (1 "   "   )
1   " Battalion Headquarters.

BY YORKSHIRE REGIMENT.

1 per platoon & 1 Battalion Headquarters.
All will report to R.E.Dump at 10-30 p.m.

No.5. Transport Officer will arrange for 1 Limber per Coy & Battalion Headquarters & Maltese Cart to report to ration dump at 10-30 p.m. 19th for Carriage of Lewis Guns etc.

No.6. Water will be drawn from Water Carts only.
Water duty men will report to Battalion Headquarters as soon as relieved by Yorkshire Water Guard.

No.7. Trench Store Lists will be handed to Orderly Room by 9 a.m. 20th inst.

No.8. Completion of relief will be reported by wire by Code J.C.
Test messages to be sent by "A" & "D" Coys before reporting.
Companies will report to Battalion Headquarters on arrival in new positions.

No.9. Patrols from front Companies in front of Company fronts will remain out during relief & until relieved by patrols of 13th Yorkshire Regiment.

                                    AuB__ Lieutenant
                                    BATTALION SUFFOLK REGIMENT. Adjt

OPERATION ORDERS

BY

LIEUT.COL. T. EARDLEY-WILMOT, D.S.O.,
COMMDG. 12TH BN. SUFFOLK REGIMENT.
:-:-:-:-:-:-:-:-:-:-:-:-:-:

June 26th, 1917.

1. The Battalion will be relieved on night 27/28th June by 17th Welsh Regiment.
   On relief the Battalion will take over billets from 18th Welsh Regiment at SOREL.

2. Advance parties of 1 Officer, 1 N.C.O. 4 Men per Company and 1 Officer 1 N.C.O. 1 Man Battalion Headquarters will report to Battalion Headquarters, 18th Welsh Regiment at 5 p.m., 27th inst. to take over stores and accommodation.
   Companies will march by Platoons at 100 yds. distance.
   Route: Track running down valley W.11.b.8.2. to HENDICOURT - SOREL.
   The 4 Men per Company and 1 Battalion Headquarters will meet their respective Platoons at W.15.c.0.8 and conduct them to billets.
   Sergt. Jones will take over Signals at SOREL.
   Water tins will be carried.

3. GUIDES. Will be found as under :-

   1 per Platoon "A" Coy. will meet "A" Coy. 17th Welsh at W.9.d.8.9. at 9.30 p.m. 27th instant.
   1 per Platoon "B" Coy. will meet "B" Coy. 17th Welsh at 9.30 p.m. at W.9.d.8.9. 27th instant.
   1 per Platoon "C" Coy. will meet "C" Coy. 17th Welsh at 9.30 p.m. at W.9.d.8.9. 27th instant.
   1 per Platoon "D" Coy. will meet "D" Coy. 17th Welsh at 9.30 p.m. at W.9.d.8.9. 27th instant.
   1 Guide Bn.H.Qrs. will meet Bn. H. Qrs. 17th Welsh at 9.30 p.m. at W.9.d.8.9. 27th instant.

   O.C. "A" Coy. will detail an Officer to superintend the Guides of all Companies.

4. The Transport Officer will arrange
   (1) To fetch all Officers Kits on night of 27th inst.
   (2) For 1 Limber per Coy. to report to Coys at 10 p.m. 27th inst.
       1 "   " Bn.H.Q.)   to report to Bn. H.Q. at
       1 Maltese Cart.   )   10 p.m. for carriage of
                                Lewis Guns, etc.

5. Trench Store Lists for both the present positions and SOREL will be sent to Orderly Room by 9 a.m. 28th inst.

6. Completion of relief will be wired to Battalion Headquarters in usual Code.

7. Baths at SOREL are allotted as under on 28th June :-

   "A" Coy.   9 a.m. to 11 a.m.
   "B" "   11 a.m. to 1 p.m.
   "C" "   1 p.m. to 3 p.m.
   "D" "   3 p.m. to 5 p.m.

   All men on Battalion Headquarters, Quarter Master Stores and Transport will bathe with their Companies.

[signature]
Lieutenant
& Adjutant,
12th Bn. Suffolk Regiment.

Appendix O

	Officers.	O.R.
Strength of Battalion on June 1st.	39	761
" " " " 30th.	37	778
Casualties during June.	Capt. A.H.M.Jackson.	31
Reinforcements during June.	3/Lieut. F.W.Leeman (Ret.from Hosp. Sick 13/6/17.	43*

* 18 had previously served with the Battalion, being evacuated through wounds or sickness. 24 were new men.

Only additional information regarding "wanting to complete," and sufficient information to explain the difference between the present and previous week's effective strength is to be entered on this side.

WAR DIARY

of

12th Bn SUFFOLK REGT

From 1/7/17

To 31/7/17

(Volume 14)

Original Copy

Demands made on this sheet should consist of personnel required from the Base only, and should not include any demands for personnel which can be completed by promotions or appointments within the unit.

Perforated Sheet giving detail of personnel and horses wanting to complete, shown on Army Form B. 213.

No. of Report _____

Detail of Wanting to Complete.	Drivers						Gunners	Smith Gunners	Range Takers	Farriers					Wheelers			Saddlers or Harness Makers	Blacksmiths	Bricklayers and Masons	Carpenters and Joiners	Fitters & Turners (R.E.)			Fitters			Electricians				Engine Drivers		Air Line Men	Permanent Line Men	Operators, Telegraph	Cablemen	Brigade Section Pioneers	General-duty Pioneers	Signallers	Instrument Repairers	Motor Cyclist	Motor Cyclist Artificers	Telephonists	Clerks	Machine Gunners	Fitters	Range Finders	Armourers	Armament Artificers		Storemen	Privates	W.O's. and N.C.O's. (by ranks) not included in trade columns			TOTAL to agree with wanting to complete		Horses			
	R.A.	R.E.	A.S.C.	Car	Lorry	Steam				Serjeans	Corporals	Shoeing, or Shoeing and Carriage Smiths	Cold Shoers	R.A.	H.T.	M.T.							Wood	Iron	R.A.	Wireless	Plumbers	Ordinary	W.T.	Signalmen	Loco.	Field																					Officers	Other Ranks		Riding	Draught	Heavy Draught	Pack
CAVALRY																																																												
R.A.																																																												
R.E.																																																												
INFANTRY																																																												
R.A.M.C.																																																												
A.O.C.																																																												
A.V.C.																																																												

Remarks :—

_____ Signature of Commander.

_____ Unit,

_____ Formation to which attached.

_____ Date of Despatch.

D. D. & I. London, E.C.
(7422) Wt. W14775/M1553 1,000,000 2/17 (E934) Forms B213/8

[P.T.O.

To be made up to and for Saturday in each week

No. of Report _____

FIELD RETURN.

Army Form B. 213

(To be furnished by all arms, services, and departments (except A.S.C. units) to the A.G.'s Office at the Base in accordance with Field Service Regulations, Part II.)

RETURN showing numbers (a) Effective strength of Unit.
(b) Rationed by Unit. _____ at _____ _____ Date.

DETAIL	Personnel			Animals						Guns and transport vehicles.													REMARKS
				Horses				Mules						Horsed		Mechanical							
	Officers	Other ranks	Natives	Riding	Draught	Heavy Draught	Pack	Large	Small	Guns, showing description	Ammunition wagons	Machine guns	Aircraft, showing description	4 Wheeled	2 Wheeled	Motor Cars	Tractors	Lorries, showing description	Trucks, showing description	Trailers	Motor Bicycles	Bicycles	Motor Ambulances	
Effective Strength of Unit......																								
Details *by Arms* attached to unit as in War Establishment :—																								
Total																								
War Establishment																								
Wanting to complete (Detail of Personnel and Horses below)																								
Surplus																								
*Attached (not to include the details shown above)............																								
Civilians :— Employed with the Unit......																								
Accompanying the Unit																								
TOTAL RATIONED.....																								

* In the case of field ambulances, hospitals or depots, the number of patients are to be included here, the names being shown in A.F.A. 36.

_____ Signature of Commander. _____ Date of Despatch.

Only additional information regarding "wanting to complete," and sufficient information to explain the difference between the present and previous week's effective strength is to be entered on this side.

WAR DIARY
of
12th Bn SUFFOLK REGT
From 1/7/17 To 31/7/17
(Volume 14)
Original Copy

Sheet 1

WAR DIARY
or
INTELLIGENCE SUMMARY
(Erase heading not required.)

12th Bn Suffolk Regt

Army Form C. 2118

Place	Date	Hour	Summary of Events and Information	Remarks and references to Appendices
MAP Ref. Sheet 57 C. S.E SOREL	JULY 1917 1		In Camp as Brigade in Reserve. aaa	Strength of Bn for June, see appendix O
"	2		" " " " " " Moved up to Front Line at VILLERS GUISLAINS & took over from 23rd MANCHESTER REGT. 35th DIV:	See appendix 1.
VILLERS GUISLAINS	3		In Front line Quiet aaa 5th Lancers on the right 15th York on the left aaa	
"	4		" " " " " aaa	
"	5		" " " " " aaa	
"	6		" " " " " aaa	
"	7		" " " " Enemy artillery activity above normal, No casualties. 35th Division took over the Sector on our right aaa	
"	8		In front line. Hostile artillery above normal aaa	
"	9		" " " Usual artillery & M.G. fire aaa	
"	10		" " " Artillery above normal aaa	
"	11		" " " Enemy fired on back areas during the day. In the early morning he obtained a few direct hits on front line trench doing small damage. No casualties. At 11.45 pm the enemy attempted to raid our extreme right post, throwing bombs in to the trench from our wire. We immediately opened fire from post with Lewis Gun & rifle fire & bombs whereon the enemy withdrew. Our Patrol which was out almost to the enemy wire hearing the bombing immediately returned & fired on the enemy as they retired, they were not able, however, to get to close quarters owing to their rapid withdrawal. aaa	aaa See appendix 2

Part II   **WAR DIARY** 12th B: Suffolk Regt   Army Form C. 2118

Instructions regarding War Diaries and Intelligence
Summaries are contained in F. S. Regs., Part II.
and the Staff Manual respectively. Title Pages
will be prepared in manuscript.

INTELLIGENCE SUMMARY

(Erase heading not required.)

Place	Date	Hour	Summary of Events and Information	Remarks and references to Appendices
VILLERS GUISLAIN	July 12		In front line Hostile artillery normal amc	
	13		" " " Quiet amc	
	14		" " " Hostile Artillery very active on front trenches amc	
	15		" " " Usual Artillery amc	
	16		" " " Patrols encountered enemy in strength + after a short engagement withdrew to our lines amc.	
	17		In front line. Quiet day. Our patrols went out as usual. A strong fighting patrol under 2Lt PASSMAN encountered a large party of the enemy + after a sharp engagement the enemy withdrew to a wired post at X.11.a.9.9 Casualties 1 missing 2 wounded. It is believed that enemy Casualties were heavy. amc	
	18		In front line Quiet. Relieved by 13th B. Yorkshire Regt + marched to Reserve with 2 Coy + HQ at VAUCELETTE FARM + 2 Coy at HEUDECOURT amc	See appendix 3
VAUCELETTE FARM.	19		In Reserve amc	
	20		" " amc	
	21		" " amc	
	22		" " amc see appendix	
	23.		" " amc	
	24		" " amc.	
	25		" " Moved into Support at VILLERS GUISLAIN. + relieved the 20th Middlesex amc	See appendix 5
VILLERS GUISLAIN	26		In Support amc.	

1875 Wt. W593/826 1,000,000 4/15 J.B.C. & A. A.D.S.S./Forms/C. 2118.

WAR DIARY *or* **INTELLIGENCE SUMMARY**

Sheet III   12th Bn Suffolk Regt   Army Form C. 2118

(Erase heading not required.)

Place	Date	Hour	Summary of Events and Information	Remarks and references to Appendices
VILLERS GUISLAIN	July 27		In Support ame	
	28		" " ame	
	29		" " ame	
	30		" " ame	
	31		" " ame	

                                                        Officers   O.R.

Strength on July 1st   37   778

Strength " " 31st   38   864

Casualties during the month   1   17.

2/Lt A.N. RUCKER Wounded 17/7/17

Reinforcements during the month   6   110

2/Lt F. ADAMS   2/Lt R.E. GOOCH   2/Lt A.W. BARNARD   2/Lt H.W. ROBINSON   16/7/17

                                      2/Lt G.R. PEDGICK   2/Lt C.H. COCKERTON   29/7/17

Officers taken off Strength during month

Major L. LLOYD   Senior Officers course England.

2/Lt A.N. RUCKER   Wounded

Lts G.R. SMITH   H.A. WHITE   B.F. MANSFIELD   Sick to England.

T. Pawsey Lt Col

Appendix 1

S E C R E T.

OPERATION ORDERS
by
MAJOR L. LLOYD,
COMMDG. 12TH. BN. SUFFOLK REGIMENT.
:-:-:-:-:-:-:-:-:-:-:-:-:-:-:-:-:

Copy No. 11.

IN THE FIELD.   July 1st, 1917.

1. The Brigade will relieve 35th Division on nights of 1/2nd July, 2/3rd July.

2. The Battalion will relieve 23rd Manchester Regiment in the Right Sub-sector on the night 2/3rd July.

3. 2 Platoons "G" Company, 12th Suffolks will relieve "X" Company 23rd Manchester Regt. on the right via VAUGUS AVENUE.
2 Platoons "G" Company, 12th Suffolks will relieve "W" Company 23rd Manchester Regt. on the left via STORAR AVENUE.
"B" Coy. 12th Suffolks will relieve "Y" Coy. 23rd Manchester Regt.
"A" Coy. 12th Suffolks will relieve "Z" Coy. 23rd Manchester Regt.
"D" Coy. 12th Suffolks will relieve a Company of the 18th Lancashire Fusiliers at VAUCELLETTE FARM.
This Company will be in Brigade Reserve under Command of Major Mason of the 21st Middlesex Regt. O.C. "D" Coy. will report to Major Mason upon his arrival.

4. On completion of relief dispositions will be as under :-

    Front Line,   "G" Coy.
    Support,   "B" "
    Bn. Reserve,   "A" "
    Bde. Reserve,   "D" "

4. Order of March.   "G", "B", "A", "D", Battalion Headquarters.
Companies will move by Platoons at 100 yards interval.
Dress. Light Fighting Order. Water bottles will be filled.
Route. HEUDICOURT - VAUCELLETTE FARM - TARGELLE RAVINE. Companies will be clear of RAILTON CROSS ROADS, W.15.d.9.0. by 9 p.m. No formed bodies of troops will move East of BROWN LINE before 9.45 p.m.

5. Guides. Guides of 23rd Manchester Regt. will be at CROSS ROADS, X.15.d.6.1. at 9.45 p.m.

    2 from "X" Coy. 23rd Manchester Regt. for 2 Right Platoons "G" Coy. 12th Suffolks.
    2 from "W" Coy. 23rd Manchester Regt. for 2 Left Platoons "G" Coy. 12th Suffolks.
    4 from "Y" Coy. 23rd Manchester Regt. for "B" Coy. 12th Suffolks.
    4 from "Z" Coy. 23rd Manchester Regt. for "A" Coy. 12th Suffolks.
    1 from Bn.Hd.Qrs.23rd Manchester Regt.for Bn.Hd.Qrs.12th Suffolks.

6. Advance party will go forward to take over Stores, Accommodation, etc. It will consist of 2nd Lieut. Hammonds, 2 N.C.Os. and 1 Signaller from "G" Coy. 1 N.C.O. and 1 Signaller from "A" Coy. 1 N.C.O. and 1 Signaller from "B" Coy. and 1 N.C.O. and 1 Signaller from Battalion Headquarters. It will be at CROSS ROADS at X.13.d.6.1. at 11 a.m. tomorrow, July 2nd, where a guide of the 23rd Manchester Regt. will meet it.

7. 20 Water tins per "A", "B", and "G" Coys. will be carried full. Camp Kettles will be taken. Rations will be taken.

8. Transport Officer will arrange for 1 limber per Company for Lewis Guns, etc. and 1 limber and Maltese cart for Battalion Headquarters.

9. Transport and Quarter Master's Stores will not move.

10. Trench Store Lists will be sent to Battalion Headquarters at completion of relief, signed by an Officer of both Battalions.

P.T.B.

11. Completion of relief will be wired by usual code.

12th. Battalion Suffolk Regiment.

Lieutenant,
A/Adjutant.

Copy No. 1. to O.C. 23rd Manchester Regt.
"   2. " O.C. 18th Lancashire Fusiliers.
"   3. " O.C. "A" Company.
"   4. " O.C. "B" Company.
"   5. " O.C. "C" Company.
"   6. " O.C. "D" Company.
"   7. " Transport Officer.
"   8. " Quartermaster.
"   9. " R.S.M.
"   10. " File.
"   11. " War Diary.
"   12. " War Diary.

Appendix 7

OPERATION ORDERS
BY
LIEUT.COL. T. EARDLEY-WILMOT, D.S.O. Copy No...9...
COMDG. 12TH. BN. SUFFOLK REGIMENT.
:-
July 10th, 1917.

1. The Brigade Front will be readjusted as follows on night 11/12th July:-

    Front Line:
        Right Sub-sector : 12th Suffolk Regiment.
        Left Sub-sector : 20th Middlesex Regt.
    Support :
        13th Yorkshire Regt.
    Reserve :
        21st Middlesex Regt.

2. The Battalion will extend its front, taking over the Sub-sector at present held by 13th Yorkshire Regt. and the post of 20th Middlesex Regt. as far South as the junction of CIRCUS TRENCH with the old front line at K5c.45-45 exclusive.

3. "A" Company Suffolks will relieve Coy. 13th Yorks in the Front Line and the post of the 20th Middlesex Regt. as far South as the junction of CIRCUS TRENCH, with the old Front Line at K5c.45-45 exclusive.
    "B" Coy. will remain as at present.
    "C" " Will relieve "A" Coy. in Support.
    "D" " Will remain as at present in Reserve.
    Battalion Headquarters will not move.

4. Upon completion of readjustment dispositions will be as follows :-
    "B" Coy.   Right Front Line.
    "A" "   Left Front Line.
    "C" "   Support.
    "D" "   Reserve.
    Bn. Hd. Qrs. Same position as at present.

5. All details of readjustment will be arranged direct between Company Commanders concerned.

6. No formed bodies of troops will cross the BROWN LINE before 9.45 p.m.

7. Advance parties from "A" and "C" Coys. will be sent to take over Stores and Accommodation in their new positions.

8. Trench Store Lists will be sent to Battalion Headquarters upon completion of relief.

9. Transport Officer will arrange for :
    (a) 1 limber for "C" Coy. to take Lewis Guns, etc;
    (b) Packs of "C" Coy. to be collected and taken to Quarter Master's Stores.
    (c) Reconnoitre the ration route to "A" Coy's. new position.

9. O.C. "A" Coy. will arrange to draw water from well in VILLERS GUISLAIN.

10. Completion of relief will be wired in usual Code.

Lieutenant
& Adjutant,
12th Bn. Suffolk Regiment.

Copy to:
1. O.C. "A" Coy.
2. O.C. "B" "
3. O.C. "C" "
4. O.C. "D" "
5. O.C. 13th Yorks.
6. Brigade Reserve.
7. Transport Officer.
8. Quarter Master.
9. War Diary.
10. War Diary.
11. File.

S E C R E T.

Appendix 3
Copy No. 10

OPERATION ORDERS
BY
LIEUT. COL. T. EARDLEY-WILMOT, D.S.O.
COMMANDING 12TH BN. SUFFOLK REGIMENT.
:-:-:-:-:-:-:-:-:-:-:-:-:-:-:-:-:-:-
July 17th, 1917.

1. The Battalion will be relieved on night of 18/19th July by Bn. Yorkshire Regt. as under :-

   "C" Coy. Yorkshires will relieve "A" Coy. Suffolks.
   "B" "   "   "   "B" "   "
   "A" "   "   "   "C" "   "
   "D" "   "   "   "D" "   "
   Hd. Qrs.   "   "   Hd. Qrs. "

2. After relief Companies will march by Platoons to billets as under and become Reserve Battalion :-

   "A" & "D" Coys. & Hd. Qrs. to VAUCELETTE FARM.
   "B" & "C"   "   "   to HENDICOURT.

3. Advance Parties of Bn. Yorkshire Regt. will arrive about 3 p.m. 18th July. Advance Parties of Bn. Suffolk Regt. consisting of 1 Officer, 1 N.C.O. and 4 men per Company and 1 N.C.O. Bn. Hd. Qrs. will report to Headquarters, Yorkshire Regt. at 3 p.m. 18th July. The 4 men will meet their respective Companies under Company arrangements and act as guides.

4. GUIDES. Guides will be provided by Bn. Suffolks as under :-
   1 Per Platoon "A" Coy. to be at Yorkshires old Headquarters HIGH ST. X 3 d 65 30 at 10 p.m. 18th instant.
   1 Per Platoon "D" Company, to be at junction of GLOSTER ROAD & LEITH WALK at 10 p.m. 18th July.
   (ii) 3 Platoons to go up by FAWCUS AVENUE and 3 Platoons by STORER AVENUE.
   1 Per Bn. Hd. Qrs. at junction of GLOSTER ROAD and LEITH WALK at 10 p.m. 18th July.
   1 Per Platoon "C" Coy. to be at junction GLOSTER ROAD and LEITH WALK at 10 p.m. July 18th.
   No Guides are required from "B" Company.

5. Trench Stores will be handed over and receipts sent to Orderly Room by 9 a.m. 19th instant.

6. Transport Officer will arrange :-
   (i) 1 Limber per Coy. & Hd. Qrs. and Maltese Cart to report to the respective ration dumps at 11 p.m. for carriage of Lewis Guns, etc.
   (ii) Water Carts to be taken out.
   (iii) Officers Kits and mens packs of "A" & "D" Coy. and Head Quarters to be taken to VAUCELETTE FARM.
   (iv) Officers Kits and mens packs of "B" & "C" Coy. to be taken to HENDICOURT.

7. All Officers will make themselves acquainted with the whole Brigade Front and routes to Right and Left Sections of Brigade Front on 19th instant. As the Battalion will be Brigade Reserve and ready to reinforce at ½ hours notice, all routes must be thoroughly known. Companies will report to Bn. Hd. Qrs. when this has been done.

8. Os.C. "A" "B" & "C" Coys. will draw their issue of Radium Sights from Q.M. Stores and fix same by 20th inst., reporting to Bn. Hd. Qrs. when this is done.

9. Arrangements for baths will be published later.

10. Completion of relief will be wired to Battalion Headquarters in usual code.

(signed) Allen
Lieutenant
& Adjutant,
12th Bn. Suffolk Regiment.

Copies to :
1. O.C. "A" Company.
2. O.C. "B" "
3. O.C. "C" "
4. O.C. "D" "
5. Transport Officer.
6. Quarter Master.
7. O.C. 13th Yorkshire Regt.
8. O.C. 21st Middlesex.
9. O.C. 23rd Manchester Regt.
10. War Diary.
11. War Diary.
12. File.

BATTALION ORDERS
BY
LIEUT.COL. T. EARDLEY-WILMOT" D.S.O.
COMMANDING BN. SUFFOLK REGIMENT.

:-:

IN THE FIELD.

Part 1.   July 22nd, 1917.

No.1. DISCIPLINE.

No man will be allowed out of his Company area without the permission of his Company Commander.

No.2. DISCIPLINE.

The Small Box Respirator will be carried by all ranks at all times.

No.3. SNIPING.

2/Lieut. H.G. Mathew is appointed Battalion Sniping Officer from 22/7/17, and will be attached to Battalion Headquarters.

Lieut. B.E. Pledger will report to "B" Company for duty pending the return of 2/Lieut. R.T. Robbins, when he will rejoin "A" Company without further orders.

No.4. TRAIN SERVICE.

With reference to Divnl. Routine Order 1309 dated 11th July 1917, a Passenger Service (Decauville) as under has been arranged with effect from 21st July. It is no charge for the journey.

	A.M.		P.M.
FINS.	9.0	(Ration Dump)	2.0
NURLU.	9.20		2.20
AIZECOURT.	9.40		2.40
QUINCONCE.	10.10		3.10
	P.M.		
QUINCONCE.	9.15		
AIZECOURT.	9.35		
NURLU.	9.55		
FINS.	10.25		

This Service will run daily unless the line is urgently required for other traffic. It is liable to be suspended without notice if the tactical situation demands it.

(Authy: III Corps Routine Order 264 dated 19/7/17).

No.5. GALLANT CONDUCT.

The Commanding Officer wishes to bring to the notice of all Ranks the Gallant Conduct of the undermentioned:-

No.27577	Sergeant	Knight, W.	"A" Coy.
27658	Private	Le Serve, W.	"
21127	"	Harris, W.	"
40320	"	Franklin, A.	"
50418	"	Jackson, G.	"
10205	"	Sherman, J.	"

A wounded man of "A" Company was in "No mans' land". The above named men volunteered to fetch him in. They crawled out 250 yds. in full view of the enemy and succeeded in bringing him in to our lines.

(Signed) A.M. CROSS, Lieutenant & Adjutant,

Battalion Suffolk Regiment.

Appendix 6

OPERATION ORDERS   Copy No. 10......

By

LIEUT.COL. T. EARDLEY-WILMOT, D.S.O.
COMDG. 12TH BN. SUFFOLK REGIMENT.
:-:-:-:-:-:-:-:-:-:-:-:-:-:-:-
July 24th, 1917.

1. The Battalion will relieve 20th Middlesex Regt. in support on night 25/26th July as under :- Marching Order.

   RELIEVED.   RELIEVING.
   "A" Coy. relieve   "B" Coy in CHURCH ROAD.
        less 2 platoons
   "B" " 2 platoons   relieve   "D" " 2 platoons by CHINESE SWITCH.
                                                "D" " 2 platoons in CHINESE ROAD.
   "D" " relieve   "A" " in GREEN LINE N.E.D.
   "D" " less 2 platoons relieve
   "C" " 2 platoons relieve   "C" " GLOSTER ROAD.
   (These two platoons must be not less)   "C" " 2 platoons in FAMOUS
   (than a total of 30 rifles and two)   Strong point.
         Lewis Guns.   )

2. Companies will find garrison trench maintenance parties as under :-

   "A" Coy.   4 men   TRENTE TWO AVENUE.
   "B" "   4 "   PAPRUS AVENUE.
   "C" "   4 "   SUNKEN AVENUE.
   "D" "   4 "   CIRCUS SWITCH.

3. GUIDES. Guides will be found by Middlesex Regt. as under :-

   4 Guides for "A" Coy. Suffolks   at CHAPEL CROSSING
   4 "   "   "B" "   "   at 11 p.m.
   1 "   "   Bn.Hd.Qrs.
   4 Guides for "D" Coy. Suffolks   at junction of GREEN
                                             LINE and LARCH WALK
                                             at 11 p.m.
   2 Guides for "C" Coy. Suffolks   at junction of GLOSTER
                                             ROAD and LARCH WALK
                                             at 11 p.m.

4. Advance Parties of 1 Officer and 1 N.C.O. per Company and Bn. Head Quarters will report to their respective Companies at 5 p.m. to Hd Qrs. 20th Middlesex Regt. at 5pm.

5. Advance Parties of Middlesex will arrive during the day to take over Stores and accommodation.

6. Trench Store lists of both positions will be sent to Adjutant by 6 p.m. 25th instant.

7. Completion of relief will be wired to Battalion Headquarters in usual code.

8. 2nd Lieut. Anther and Snipers will remain at HEDICOURT for further training.

9. Transport Officer will arrange for :-

   1 Limber to report to each Company for Carriage of Lewis Guns, rations, etc.
   1 Limber and Maltese Cart to Bn. Hd. Qrs. Water Carts will be sent up one to "A" & "B" Coys. and one to "D" & "C" Coys.

                                    [signature] Lieutenant
                                                 & Adjutant,
                                    12th Battalion Suffolk Regiment.

Copy No: 1 to O.C. "A" Coy.
2 " O.C. "B" "
3 " O.C. "C" "
4 " O.C. "D" "
5 " 2nd Lt. H.C. Mathew.
6 " Transport Officer.
7 " Quarter Master,
8 " R.S.M.
9 " O.C. 20th Middlesex.
10 " War Diary.
11 " War Diary.
12 " File.

WAR DIARY of 15th Bn SUFFOLK REGT

From 1/8/17 To 31/8/17

(Volume 18)

Original

Perforated Sheet giving detail of personnel and horses wanting to complete, shown on Army Form B. 213.

Number of Report _____

Detail of Wanting to Complete	Drivers						Gunners	Smith Gunners	Range Takers	Farriers			Cold Shoers	Wheelers			Saddlers or Harness Makers	Blacksmiths	Bricklayers and Masons	Carpenters and Joiners	Fitters & Turners (R.E.)		Fitters		Plumbers	Electricians			Signalmen	Engine Drivers			Air Line Men	Permanent Line Men	Operators, Telegraph	Cablemen	Brigade Section Pioneers	General-duty Pioneers	Signallers	Instrument Repairers	Motor Cyclists	Motor Cyclist Artificers	Telephonists	Clerks	Machine Gunners	Armament Artificers		Armourers	Storemen	Privates	W.O's. and N.C.O's. (by ranks) not included in trade columns			TOTAL to agree with wanting to complete		Horses			
	R.A.	R.E.	A.S.C.	Car	Lorry	Steam				Sergeants	Corporals	Shoeing, or Shoeing and Carriage Smiths		R.A.	H.T.	M.T.					Wood	Iron	R.A.	Wireless		Ordinary	W.T.		Loco.	Field															Fitters	Range Finders								Officers	Other Ranks	Riding	Draught	Heavy Draught	Pack
CAVALRY																																																										
R.A.																																																										
R.E.																																																										
INFANTRY																																																										
R.A.M.C.																																																										
A.O.C.																																																										
A.V.C.																																																										

Remarks:—

_____ Signature of Commander.

_____ Unit.

_____ Formation to which attached.

_____ Date of Despatch.

[P.T.O.

WAR DIARY or INTELLIGENCE SUMMARY

Army Form C. 2118

August 1917

Place	Date	Hour	Summary of Events and Information	Remarks and references to Appendices
VILLERS GUISLAIN	1		In Support B'n. HQ at X.16.90.05. with 2 Companies at X.16.B.1. One Company at X.15.d.87, + one at X.15.c.2.1 + X.15.d.1.9. 2 Lewis gun pack mule sections in the reserve line "Gouzencourt (B.)" Have one Lewis gun from 2/O'MIDDLESEX R.3 + 4.5.7. + R.3.a.8.5. Wajr 5.7.c.5.E on W.53.d.	Appendix 1
GONNELIEU	2		Reorganise in show. At night one Lewis Gun from 1/8 Argylls from R.34.b.5.7. + R.3.0. 8.3. 20/MIDDLESEX on right over 13 + Sw.13 & Left.	Appendix 2
	3		2/Lt Al GRIFFITHS killed on patrol in the early morning. Quiet. In front lines.	
	4		Quiet. 2/Lt T ROBINS awarded M.C.	Appendix 3
	5		Quiet. Very little activity.	
	6		Quiet	
	7		Quiet	
	8		Quiet	
	9		Quiet. One team extra duties.	
	10		Very little activity	
	11		Quiet. At night relieved by 13th Yorks + moved into Bde Reserve with 2 Coys at VAUCELLETTE FARM – X.13.c – and 2 Coys at HEUDICOURT	
VAUCELLETTE FARM	12		In Bde Reserve	
	13		" "	
	14		" "	

WAR DIARY ~~INTELLIGENCE SUMMARY~~

Sheet 2.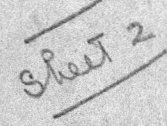

Army Form C. 2118.

12th Bn. Suffolk Regt.

Place	Date	Hour	Summary of Events and Information	Remarks and references to Appendices
VAUCELETTE FARM	15		In Bde. Reserve. At night relieved ~~13th Yorks~~ 20th Mx in Support. Hq. & 2 Coys at X3C 0-9 a. 2 Coys. at R26d. MM	Appendix 4
	16		In Support as above MM	
	17		" " " " MM	
	18		" " " " MM	
	19		" " " " At night relieved 13th Yorks in the line MM	Appendix 5
GONNELIEU	20		In the line as left Bn. at GONNELIEU. Front very quiet MM	
	21		" " " " " " " MM	
	22		" " " " " " " Concentrations by our Artillery drew a few shells from enemy three falling amongst our patrol. 2 Lt. Tricker wounded and 6 OR wounded MM	
	23		In the line as left Bn. at GONNELIEU MM	
	24		" " " " " " MM	
	25		" " " " " " : We exploded 2 Bangalore torpedoes in enemy wire MM	
	26		In front line. Quiet. AMC	
	27		" " Quiet. Relieved by 13th Bn YORKSHIRE REGT & moved to Reserve AMC	Appendix 6
VAUCELETTE FARM	28		In Reserve AMC	

			WAR DIARY or INTELLIGENCE SUMMARY.	Army Form C. 2118.

Instructions regarding War Diaries and Intelligence Summaries are contained in F. S. Regs., Part II. and the Staff Manual respectively. Title pages will be prepared in manuscript.

Sheet 3

(Erase heading not required.)

12th Bn Suffolk Regt

Place	Date	Hour	Summary of Events and Information	Remarks and references to Appendices
	Aug.			
VAUCELETTE FARM	29		In Reserve. AMC	
	30		" " AMC	
	31		" " Relieved the 20th MIDDLESEX in Support. AMC	See appendix 1.
			Strength on 1st 40 Off 867 O.R.	
			" " 31st 45 " 855 "	
			Casualties during month 2/Lt A.I. GRIFFITHS Killed 3/8/17	
			2/Lt R. TRICKER wounded, at duty 23/8/17	
			1 OR Killed 14 OR Wounded.	
			Reinforcements 9 Officers 13 O.R.	
			2/Lts J. FRYETT, R.F.FRANCIS., F.T.VERRY, H.L.CHIPPINGTON, F.W.SPURGEON	
			K. PEARCE W.E. WHYMARK J.T. SUTTLE, E.C.SHARP	
			[signature]	
			Comdg 12 Bn Suffolk Regt	

T2134. Wt. W708—776. 500000. 4/15. Sir J. C. & S.

SECRET.

DEFENCE SCHEME.

LEFT BATTALION - 121ST INFANTRY BRIGADE.
----

1. The Battalion defends GONNELIEU Village and Ridge. It holds a continuous Front Line from GIN AVENUE on left at R.27.a.7.4. to TURNERS QUARRY, exclusive. An advanced line is under construction on the other flank, R.26.c. and then the two roads leading to R.27.c.9.4. but is not held except that portion known as NEWTONS POST round the road junction at R.34.a.7.7.

2. GENERAL CHARACTERISTICS OF SECTION AND COMMUNICATION.

The whole Section is commanded by GONNELIEU RIDGE and VILLAGE. NEWTONS POST sweeps the wire between it and TURNERS QUARRY and CHESHIRE STREET, the GONNELIEU VACQUERIE ROAD and the GONNELIEU BANTEUX ROAD cut up the Front into 3 distint Sectors.

The chief communications are :-

Left. GIN AVENUE.
Road. R.26.d.9.5. to R.27.a.b.3.

Centre.
Road. R.26.c.9.1. eastwards through Village - past church - and then the two roads leading to R.27.c.9.4. and R.27.d.4.4. and to R.27.d.0.2 and then via GRESHAM STREET to Front Line.

Right.
Roads to R.27.d.0.2. and onwards via GRESHAM AVENUE.
Track. R.33.a.3.4 to R.33.b.5.4 and thence to Front line via WILLIS AVENUE.

Via KITCHEN CRATER and 22 RAVINE or CHESHIRE QUARRY and BICESTER AVENUE.

In the event of entry by the enemy, these communication trenches could be manned and a defensive flank formed.

3. The Front line is to be held at all costs, and if entered by the enemy a counter-attack from the flanks and rear will be launched immediately. If this does not succeed, the point of entry should be localized by holding the enemy in a pocket and preventing him extending his gains. A counter-attack with an artillery preparation will then be launched by the Reserve Battalion.

4. DISTRIBUTION.

Left Front Coy. From GIN AVENUE to BOYEAU 1 (R.27.c.8.0) inclusive.

Right Front Coy. From BOYEAU 1 (R.27.c.8.0) exclusive to TURNERS QUARRY exclusive.

Left Support Coy. 1 Platoon GUN Support (R.27a.3.0) (close support). 3 Platoons in Reserve Line.
R.26.c.9.6.

Right Support Coy. 1 Platoon in road about R.33.b.6.5 (close support).
2 Platoons in and about KITCHEN CRATER.
1 Platoon in Sunken Road R.33.a.2.7.

Snipers. In cellars in Brewery. R.32.b.9.7.

Support Battalion. Battalion Headquarters R.26.d.4.7.
3 Platoons in Reserve Line. R.32.b. near QUENTIN MILL K.1.b.
1 Company in Reserve Line.

In addition to above, 2 Platoons of the Right Battalion are in CHESHIRE QUARRY and 1 Platoon in CROOKS QUARRY.

(Contd).

SHEET II.

5. **ACTION IN CASE OF RAID OR HEAVY BOMBARDMENT.**

S.O.S. rocket is a rifle grenade bursting into 2 red and 2 white stars, and should be sent up only when enemy are seen advancing to the attack.
In case of heavy bombardment, troops should be withdrawn to each side of the barrage. Lewis Gunners and Riflemen should be pushed forward on each flank and every effort made to enfilade the enemy should he attempt to raid under cover of the bombardment.
This does not apply to Newton Post, which must be held at all costs.

Os.C. Coys. in Front Line will immediately telephone to the battery covering them and to Battalion Headquarters.

All troops in the Sub-section will 'stand to' in battle order and Os.C. Coys. will get in touch with the situation.

Working Parties in Front Line will 'stand to' and man fire bays reporting to the nearest Company Headquarters.

Right Support 2 Platoons at KITCHEN CRATER will move to junction of road and track at R.33.a.7.5, sending an Officer to Right Coy. Headquarters.

Right Support Platoon at R.33.a.2.6 and snipers will 'stand to' and move into GRESHAM AVENUE - putting a Lewis Gun and team and bombers in the block of GRESHAM AVENUE.

Left Support 3 Platoons will move up GIN ALLEY as far as CEMETERY ROAD and send forward an Officer to Left Coy. Headquarters.
The Company of Support Battalion at X.1.b. will move to Reserve Line at R.26.c.9.6.
If S.O.S. Grenade is fired, the artillery put down a barrage 150 yards in Front of our wire.

Counter preparations can also be called for, which means a barrage on the enemys' front line. The following counter preparations are in force, and will be called for immediately if enemy bombards Front Line heavily.

    Counter preparation A - R.28.d.12 to R.28.a.1.1.
                "   B - R.28.a.11 to R.22.c.9.6.

S.O.S. grenades (several) will be carried behind the officer on duty in Front Line. They will be carried by day as well as night. The telephone must also be used and Officers will keep a message written out at all times in the Front Line.
The S.O.S. grenade, if fired in the Front Line, will be repeated by the Company Headquarters concerned.
In event of telephone breaking down, runners must be extensively used as early information is of the utmost importance,

6. **GAS ATTACK.**

    Cloud Gas. Gongs will be beaten, strombus horns sounded, all men will wear respirators, Battalion Headquarters and artillery must be informed at once by runner or phone.

    Shell Gas. Rattles will be sounded, all men will wear respirators, Battalion Headquarters and artillery will be informed.

(Contd).

SHEET III.

7. **MACHINE GUNS & TRENCH MORTARS** are as follows :-

Machine Guns.

No. of Gun.	Location.	S.O.S. Lines Magnetic Bearing.	Range
M.G.1	R.27.d.55.05	90°	600 yds.
M.G.2	R.27.d.10.33	102°	700 "
M.G.3	R.27.d.35.85	112°	450 "
M.G.4	R.27.b.05.30	(535°	300 "
		28°	
M.G.8	X.3a.80.35	R.28.a.00.60 } S.O.S.LINES	
L.3	R.35.d.55.70	R.35.a.25.15	1500

Trench Mortars.

No.	Location.	S.O.S. Line.
3	R.27.d.30.50	R.27.d.70.80
4	R.27.c.70.70	R.27.b.10.40

8. Company Commanders will immediately prepare plans based on these orders. These will be submitted to Battalion Headquarters for approval. All ranks must know them and all Officers and N.C.Os. must have an intimate knowledge of the whole Sub-sector. Company Commanders should know the orders of the Companies on their flanks.

9. Nothing in these Orders will prevent Officers and N.C.Os. from showing iniative and taking any steps the occasion may demand if there is no time to communicate with Battalion Headquarters.

In any case, Battalion Headquarters must be informed immediately by runner and telephone of any action taken and of the local situation.

August 3rd, 1917.

[signature]
for Lieut. Col.
Commanding 12th Battalion Suffolk Regt.

Appendix 1   Copy No....

SECRET.

OPERATION ORDERS
by
LIEUT. COL. T. BARCLEY-WILMOT, D.S.O.
COMDG. 12TH BN. SUFFOLK REGIMENT.
:-:-:-:-:-:-:-:-:-:-:-:-:-:

August 1st, 1917.

1. The following reliefs will take place tonight 1st/2nd August :-

"B" Coy. will relieve part of "C" Coy. 21st Middlesex Regt. in the Front and Support Line from TURPIN'S QUARRY to SNIPERS POST, both exclusive, and "D" Coy. 21st Middlesex Regt. in GLASS STREET and KITCHEN CRATER.

Company Headquarters will be at KITCHEN CRATER but O.C. "B" Coy. will arrange, in case of emergency in Front Line, to telephone from CROSS POST QUARRY either to Company Headquarters at KITCHEN CRATER or to Battalion Headquarters at CROSS POST via late 21st Middlesex Battalion Headquarters at HIGH STREET.

An Officer will always be on duty in Front Line and in GLASS STREET.

Rations will be delivered to KITCHEN CRATER for "B" Coy. 25 full water tins will be delivered with rations for "B" Coy. Empty water tins will be dumped at Battalion Headquarters by 8 P.M. today.

2. "D" Company (2 Platoons) will move to CROSS POINT.

3. "C" Company, after relief at FAMOUS Strong Point by the Lancashire Fusiliers will move to billets at MORRIS RAW K.7.2.5.6. and IRVINE LANE W.11.4.

4. The Battalion will be distributed as under on night of 1st/2nd August :-

Battalion Hd. Qrs.   CROSS POST.
"A" & "D" Coys.   MORRIS RAW and IRVINE LANE.
"C" Company   Front Line.
"B"   "A" Company Right Support.
                       "B"   Left.

5. On night of 2nd/3rd August, the Battalion will relieve 17th Welsh in GOUZEAUCU Sector.

"B" Company in Right.   "A" Company Right Support.
"C"   " Left.   "B"   "   Left.

Os.C. Companies will arrange to reconnoitre accordingly.

6. After relief the Battalion Boundaries are as under :-

South Boundary.   TURNER'S QUARRY.
North   "   Junction of KEW ALLEY and Front Line.

(signed) ....
Lieutenant
& Adjutant,
12th Battalion Suffolk Regiment.

Copy to : 1 O.C. "A" Company.   10. R.S.M.
           2 O.C. "B"   "   11. War Diary.
           3 O.C. "C"   "   12. War Diary.
           4 O.C. "D"   "
           5 O.C. 13th Yorkshire Regt.
           6 O.C. 21st Middlesex Regt.
           7 Transport Officer.
           8. Quarter Master.
           9. Headquarters.

Appendix X

SECRET.   Copy No........

OPERATION ORDER.
BY
LIEUT. COL. F. LARDNER-CLIFTON, D.S.O.,
COMDG. 12TH BN. SUFFOLK REGIMENT.
:-:-:-:-:-:-:-:-:-:-:-:-:-:-:-:-:-:-:-

August 2nd, 1917.

1. With reference to Operation Order, para 5, dated 1/8/17, the details of relief of the 114th Brigade are as under :-

"B" Coy. Will take over Right Front Coy. of 15th Welsh Regiment. - Guides to be arranged between Companies concerned.

"C" Coy. Will take over Left Front Coy. of 15th Welsh Regt. Guides will be at ration dump at 10.15 p.m.

"A" Coy. Right Support. - Guides will be at KITCHEN GRATER at 10.30 p.m.

"D" Coy. Left Support. - Guides will be at toll in CORNHILL at 11 p.m.

2. "A" Coy. will detail 1 Platoon as Local Support to "B" Coy. They will be billeted near "B" Coy. Headquarters.

"A" Coy. will detail a fighting patrol of 1 Officer and 1 Platoon to patrol "B" Coys front.

3. Snipers will be billeted in Brewery, CORNHILL, under 2/Lieut. M. Leeming. They will report to ration dump at 10 p.m. 2/Lieut. Leeming will arrange for accommodation.

4. Signallers for Headquarters and Water Duty men will take over from 15th Welsh Regiment at 9 p.m.

5. Advance Parties of 1 Officer & 1 N.C.O. per Coy. and Headquarters will report to Battalion Headquarters, 15th Welsh Regiment, at 7.30 p.m.

6. Limbers for "A" & "D" Coys. and Headquarters will proceed via BUNNY TRAIL & GLASS STREET to CORNHILL.

7. Rations for "B" & "C" Coys. will be delivered to the respective Coy. Headquarters by "D" Coy.

8. Watering will be carried out.
   "A" Coy. will provide water party for "B" Coy.

[signature]

Lieutenant
& Adjutant,
12nd Battalion Suffolk Regiment.

Copy to 1. O.C. "A" Company.
         2. "   "B"   "
         3. "   "C"   "
         4. "   "D"   "
         5. Transport Officer.
         6. Quarter Master.
         7. O.C. 15th Welsh Regt.
         8. O.C. Right Battalion.
         9. Headquarters.
        10. R.S.M.
        11. War Diary.
        12. War Diary.
        13. 2/Lieut. Leeming.

War Diary Appendix 3

Copy No. 1.

SECRET.

OPERATION ORDERS
BY
LIEUT. COL. T. BARDLEY-WILMOT, D.S.O.
COMMANDING 12TH BN. SUFFOLK REGT.

August 10th, 1917.

1. The Battalion will be relieved on night of 11th/12th August by Bn, Yorkshire Regt. as under :-

   YORKSHIRE
   "D" Coy. will relieve "A" Coy. in Right Front.
   "C"   "   "   "D" "   " Left   "
   "B"   "   "   "B" "   " Right Support.
   "A"   "   "   "C" "   " Left Support.

   SUFFOLK
   "A" Coy. in Right Front.
   "D" "   " Left   "
   "B" "   " Right Support.
   "C" "   " Left Support.

   "A" & "B" Coys. Yorkshire Regt. will detail 1 Platoon each to take over local support from "B" & "A" Coys. Suffolk Regt. respectively.

2. GUIDES will be found by Companies as under :-

   "A" Company   2 Guides for Front Line.
   "B"   "   1   "   : Local Support.
   "D"   "   2   "   : Front Line.
   "C"   "   1   "   : Local Support.

   Snipers   1 Guide.
   "B" Company   2   "
   "C"   "   2   "
   Bn. Hd. Qrs. 1   "

   All guides will report to 2nd Lieut. Hamblin at Battalion Headquarters at 9 p.m.

3. 2nd Lieut. Hamblin will be in charge of guides and meet Bn. Yorkshire Regt. at junction of 22 AVENUE and GLASS STREET at 9.45 p.m. 11th inst.

4. When relieved the Battalion will march to Reserve as under :-

   Bn. Hd. Qrs.   VAUCELETTE FARM.
   "A" Company   HEUDECOURT X Roads
   "B"   "   VAUCELETTE FARM. Sunken Road
   "C"   "   Sunken Road
   "D"   "

5. Advance parties of Bn. Yorkshire Regt. will arrive during the afternoon of 11th instant to take over Stores, etc.

6. Advance Parties of 1 Officer & 1 N.C.O. per Company and Headquarters, Suffolk Regt. will report to Yorkshire Regt. at 5 p.m. 11th instant.

7. Trench Stops lists will be handed to Adjutant by 9 a.m. 11th inst.

8. Snipers Suits (6) will be handed over as Trench Stores.

9. Completion of relief will be wired to Battalion Headquarters by usual Code.

10. Baths will be allotted later.

Lieutenant
& Adjutant.
12th Battalion Suffolk Regt.

Copy No. 1 to O.C. "A" Company.
"   " 2 " O.C. "B"   "
"   " 3 " O.C. "C"   "
"   " 4 " O.C. "D"   "
"   " 5 " O.C. 13th Yorkshire Regt.
"   " 6 " O.C. Right Battalion.
"   " 7 " O.C. Left Battalion.
"   " 8 " Transport Officer.
"   " 9 " Quarter Master.
"   " 10 " Headquarters.
"   " 11 " R.S.M.
"   " 12 " War Diary.
"   " 13 " War Diary.
"   " 14 " Sniping Officer.

Operation Orders Appendix 4

Lieut. Col. F.G. Barclay, W.Dings D.S.O.
Comdg. 12th Bn Suffolk Regt.
                                    14th August 1917

1) The Battalion will relieve 14th & 20th
   Middlesex Regts in support on night of
   15/16th August.

2) 12th Suffolks.   20th Middlesex
   A Coy relieves relieves   Regt in CONNELLIEU
   C "   "   "   C Coy " CONNELLIEU
   B "   "   "   A " at CROSS POST
   D "   "   "   B " at CROSS POST

3) Guides. No Guides will be provided
   for D and B Companies.
   A) Guides for platoons of A Company
   Rendezvous from 20th Middlesex Regt
   near the at RUAKRY (R3.c.9.7) at
   9.30 pm 15th inst, for A and C Companies
   10 – Suffolks

4) Order of March. A.C.B.D. Coys. Bn.
   Headquarters, Coy transport in rear
   of platoons at 100 yards interval.
   Platoons feel ordinarily with guide files.
   DRESS:- Full marching order (with Packs).
   Water Bottles will be filled.

5. Movement 10 Armies. Northern 5 Armies moves into Pas de Calais. BROWN LINE before 9 Jan.

6. Reserve Italian about 20 Armies to be re-inforced during December to strength under:—
Lippes 160 Per Company and
Carbines 30 " " " "
the others the same as on the 20th.
The efforts will arrive there about the 15th to the new Reconcentration.

7. Divisions Plus 1st Transport Plus fois Armies:—
   (a) 30 battle trains to Carbines in their regiments.
   (b) Lines in the regiments.
   (c) 1 Die Larger Battery for Louis Battery.
   (d) Machinists to the Batteries.
   (e) Machinists to the Batteries.

8. Apres Charlot sera dans le Central his prolongation Brussels of Belgium et a la grandeur the Bataille.

Sheet III.

9 Completion of relief will be wired by usual code.

[illegible]

Lieutenant
a/Adjutant
12 Bn Sussex Regiment

Operation Orders Appendix 5

by

Lieut. Col. T. Pretor-Pinney D.S.O.
Commanding 12th Bn. Suffolk Regt.

Aug. 18th 1917.

1. The Battalion will relieve the 13th Yorkshire Regt. in the line on night of 19th/20th August.

2. The 13th Yorks. have 3 Coys. in the Line. Disposition of Suffolks will be as follows :-
   2 Coys. in the Line -

   "D" Coy. Right Front Line.
   "A" "   Left Front Line.

   Boundaries as last tour in the line.

   "B" Coy. Right Support.
   1 Platoon in CHESHIRE QUARRY under an officer
   1 Platoon in Close Support in McVEAGH STREET.
   2 Platoons + Coy. Hd. Qrs. in KITCHEN CRATER.

   "C" Coy. Left Support.
   1 Platoon in Close Support in GUN SUPPORT.
   3 Platoons + Coy. Hd. Qrs. in Reserve Line, as before.

3/

Sheet 4

3. No guides will be provided. Reconnaissance to commence at 9 P.M.; boys going in the front lines wearing front Dress; Full Marching Order (with belts). Water Bottles will be carried full.

4. <u>Advance Parties of 1 Officer + 1 S.N.C.O. per Coy + 1 Officer + 1 S.N.C.O. per Bn. Hd. Qrs. will go forward to take over Stores, Ammunition, etc.</u>

5. Snipers will be recommended at the Brewery + will rendezvous there on Sept 10.30 p.m. C.O. Snipers will report to Bn. Hd. Qrs. on 19th inst. at 6 p.m.

6. Transport Officer will arrange:-
   (a) To deliver rations to Coys in their new positions.
   (b) 1 limber Coy for "A" + "B" Coys + 1 limber for "C" + "D" Coys. So limbers will be required for "A" + "C" Coys.
   (c) 1 G.S. Wagon + all tools etc for Battalion Hd. Qrs.
   (d) Water cart to be taken to KITCHEN CRATER full. He will arrange for this cart to be filled nightly from VILLERS GUISLAIN.

H.

Sheet III

6. (a)(contd.) The other water cart will be taken back to Transport Lines.
   (c) If Officers wish to return their kits, they will be sent down by ration limber.

7. Movement in GLASS STREET will be reduced to a minimum.

8. Trench Store lists will not be rendered.

9. Completion of relief will be wired by code :- E.W.

Lieutenant
& Adjutant,
12th Bn. Suffolk Regt.

War Diary
Appendix 6

Operation Orders
by
Lieut. Col. T. E. Lordy Wilmington DSO
Commdg. 12th Bn. Suffolk Regt.
Aug. 26th 1917.

1. The Battalion will be relieved on night of 27/28th August by ---- Bn. Yorkshire Regt. as under:-

   "A" Coy.   Yorkshire Regt.   "C" Coy.
   "B"   "   "   "   "D" "
   "C"   "   "   "   "A" "
   "D"   "   "   "   "B" "

   No Guides required.

2. On relief the Battalion will be in Reserve as under:-

   "A" Coy.   Square HEIDICOURT.
   "D" "   X Roads,
   "B" "   Sunken Road VAUCELETTE FARM.
   "C" "   VAUCELETTE FARM.
   Hd.Qrs.   HEIDICOURT.
   Snipers   "

3. Advance Parties of 1 Officer & 1 N.C.O. per Company & Headquarters will report to Bn. Hd. Qrs. Yorkshire Regt. at 5 p.m. 27th inst.

4. Trench Stores will be handed over & receipts sent to Orderly Room by 9 a.m. 28th inst.

5. Transport Officer will arrange for:-
   1 Officers' mess Company's kit & not (?) 1 Limbers Mather Cart to report to
   Battalion dumps for carriage of Lewis Guns, etc.

6. Completion of relief will be wired in usual code.

   A. W. Cox
   Adjutant
   12th Bn. Suffolk Regt.

Appendix 7

Operation Orders
by
Major F.L. Mashiter,
Comm'd'g 12th Bn. Suffolk Regt.   August 31st 1917.

1. The Battalion will relieve the 20th Middlesex Regt. on night 31st August/1st Sept in Support.
   The 20th Middlesex will take over as Reserve Bn.

2. Companies will relieve as under:-

   12th Suffolk   20th Middlesex
   "A" Company   relieves   "D" Company
   "B"   "   "   "C"   "
   "C"   "   "   "B"   "
   "D"   "   "   "A"   "

   "D" Coy. will detail 1 Platoon of 1 Officer & 25 O.R. to live at KITCHEN CRATER.

3. Advance Parties of 1 Officer & 1. & 8.20 per Coy. & 2 Lewis Gun & Lewis Gun N.C.O. from Hd. Qrs. will report to Bn. Hd. Qrs. 20th Middlesex Regt. at 5 p.m. to take over stores etc.

4. Advance Parties of 20th Middlesex Regt. will report during the afternoon.

5. The right for French Stores will be carried to Vandenberghe Farm at 1st September.

6. Completion of relief will be reported by usual code.

7. The Quartermaster will arrange for:-
   (a) Water & rations to be delivered to new position
   (b) 1 Limber per Coy. & 1 Limber & Mess Cart for Bn. Hd. Qrs. at 7 p.m. Tonight 31st inst.

(Sgd) A.M. CROSS, Lieut.
Adjutant
12th Bn. Suffolk Regiment.

For information of the A.G.'s Office at the Base.

Officers and men who have become casuals, been transferred or joined since last report.

Place .... Date ....

Regtl. Number	Rank	Name	Corps	Nature of casualty, or name of unit from or to which transferred	Date of being struck off or coming on the ration return	Remarks*

* State whether absence is of a permanent or temporary nature, adding, in the case of casuals from wounds or disease, any available information for communication to the relatives.

To be made up to and for Sunday in each week.

No. of Report_____

FIELD RETURN.

Army Form B. 213.

(To be furnished by all arms, services, and departments (except A.S.C. units) to the A. G.'s Office at the Base in accordance with Field Service Regulations, Part II.)

RETURN showing numbers   (a) Effective strength of Unit.
                 (b) Rationed by Unit.   at _____ _____ Date.

DETAIL	Personnel			Animals.									Guns, carriages, and limbers and transport vehicles												Motor Bicycles	Bicycles	REMARKS
				Horses				Mules									Horsed				Mechanical							
	Officers	Other ranks	Natives	Riding	Draught	Heavy Draught	Pack	Large	Small	Camels	Oxen	Guns, carriages and limbers, showing description	Ammunition wagons and limbers	Machine guns	Aircraft, showing description	4 wheeled	2 wheeled	Motor Cars.	Tractors	Lorries, showing description	Trucks, showing description	Trailers			
Effective Strength of Unit																									
Details, *by Arms* attached to unit as in War Establishment:—																									
Total																									
War Establishment																									
Wanting to complete (Detail of Personnel and Horses below)																									
Surplus																									
*Attached (not to include the details shown above)																									
Civilians:— Employed with the Unit																									
Accompanying the Unit																									
TOTAL RATIONED...																									

* In the case of field ambulances, hospitals or depots, the number of patients are to be included here, the names being shown in A. F. A. 36.

_____ Signature of Commander.

_____ Date of Despatch.

Vol 16

WAR DIARY
1st Bn of SUFFOLK
From 1/9/17
To 30/9/17
(Volume 16)

Original

Perforated Sheet giving detail of personnel and horses wanting to complete, shown on Army Form B. 213.

Number of Report _____

Detail of Wanting to Complete	Drivers						Gunners	Smith Gunners	Range Takers	Farriers		Shoeing, or Shoeing and Carriage Smiths	Cold Shoers	Wheelers			Saddlers or Harness Makers	Blacksmiths	Bricklayers and Masons	Carpenters and Joiners	Fitters & Turners (R.E.)		Fitters		Plumbers	Electricians		Signalmen	Engine Drivers		Air Line Men	Permanent Line Men	Operators, Telegraph	Cablemen	Brigade Section Pioneers	General-duty Pioneers	Signallers	Instrument Repairers	Motor Cyclists	Motor Cyclist Artificers	Telephonists	Clerks	Machine Gunners	Armament Artificers		Armourers	Storemen	Privates	W.O's. and N.C.O's. (by ranks) not included in trade columns		TOTAL to agree with wanting to complete	Horses				
	R.A.	R.E.	A.S.C.	Car	Lorry	Steam				Serjeants	Corporals			R.A.	H.T.	M.T.					Wood	Iron	R.A.	Wireless		Ordinary	W.T.		Loco.	Field															Fitters	Range Finders						Officers	Other Ranks	Riding	Draught	Heavy Draught	Pack
CAVALRY																																																										
R.A.																																																											
R.E.																																																											
INFANTRY																																																											
R.A.M.C.																																																											
A.O.O.																																																											
A.V.C.																																																											

Remarks:— _____ Signature of Commander.

_____ Unit.

_____ Formation to which attached.

_____ Date of Despatch.

(B 99511.) Wt. W15519/M149. 1,000,000. 1/16. J. P. & Co., Ltd. Forms/B. 213/7. [P.T.O.

WAR DIARY or **INTELLIGENCE SUMMARY**

Sheet 1   12th Bn Suffolk Regt   Army Form C. 2118.

Place	Date	Hour	Summary of Events and Information	Remarks and references to Appendices
	Sept			
GONNELIEU	1		In Support to GONNELIEU Sector Quiet A.W.C.	
"	2		" " " " " Quiet	
"	3		" " " " " Quiet	
"	4		" " " " " Quiet. Relieved 13th Bn YORKSHIRE REGT in Front line 20th MIDDLESEX on right 119th Brigade on left A.W.C	See Appendix 1
"	5		In Front line. Enemy snipers more active than previously A.W.C.	
"	6		" " " Hostile artillery active A.W.C	
"	8		" " " Quiet A.W.C	
"	9		" " " Quiet A.W.C	
"	10		" " " Quiet A.W.C	
"	11		" " " Quiet A.W.C	
"	12		" " " Relieved by 13th YORKSHIRE REGT Moved to Reserve A.W.C	See Appendix II
PANCELETTE FARM	13		In Reserve. A.W.C	
"	14		" " A.W.C	
"	15		" " A.W.C	
"	16		" Relieved 20th MIDDLESEX in Support A.W.C	See Appendix III

WAR DIARY
or
INTELLIGENCE SUMMARY.
(Erase heading not required.)

Sheet II   13th Bn Suffolk Regt.

Army Form C. 2118.

Instructions regarding War Diaries and Intelligence
Summaries are contained in F. S. Regs., Part II.
and the Staff Manual respectively. Title pages
will be prepared in manuscript.

Place	Date	Hour	Summary of Events and Information	Remarks and references to Appendices
	Sept 1917			
GONNELIEU	17		In Support quiet AAA	
	18		" " " AAA	
	19		" " " relieved by 21st MIDDLESEX & moved to Reserve AAA	Appendix 4
VAUCELETTE FARM.	20		In reserve AAA	
	21		" " AAA	
	22		" " AAA	
	23		" " Relieved 13th YORKSHIRE REGT in front line AAA	Appendix 5
GONNELIEU	24		In front line 20th MIDDLESEX on the right 119th BRIGADE on the left. Quiet AAA	
GONNELIEU	25		" " " Artillery very active all day. At 7.30 pm we raided the enemy trenches in R28d. bringing back 1 light machine gun & 5 prisoners AAA	Appendix A " B
	26		Quiet. Slight shelling AAA	
	27		Quiet AAA	
	28		Quiet AAA	
	29		Quiet AAA	
	30		Slight Shelling. One battery heavily shelled with 5.9s AAA	

T 2134. Wt. W708—776. 500000. 4/15. Sir J. C. & S.

Sheet III   WAR DIARY or INTELLIGENCE SUMMARY.   12th Bn Suffolk Regt

Place	Date	Hour	Summary of Events and Information	Remarks and references to Appendices

Strength Sept 1st   Officers 45   OR 855
"   "   30th   37   882

Casualties during month of September   *Officers 5   OR 99
Reinforcements "   "   "   "   —   130

*Officer Casualties
    Capt M.E.H. SCHIFF   Missing
    2/Lt R.T. ROBINS M.C.   Wounded ⎫
    "   G HALLSMITH   "   ⎬ 26th
    "   J.T. SUTTLE   " |
    "   J FRYETT   "   ⎭

              Frank Mitchison Major
              Comdg 12th Bn Suffolk Regt.

Appendix 1

Operation Orders,
by
Major F. Miskin,
Commdg. 12th Bn. Suffolk Regt.
Sept. 3rd, 1917.

1. The Battalion will relieve the 13th Yorkshire Regt. in the Front Line on night of 4th/5th Sept. as under:-

Suffolks		Yorks	
"B" Coy.	will relieve	"B" Coy.	in Right Front.
"C" "	" "	"C" "	Left
"D" "	" "	"D" "	Right Support.
"A" "	" "	"A" "	Left "

Snipers will take over billets in Cherisy.
Guides N.L.
1 Platoon of "D" Coy. will act as Local Support to "B" Coy.
1 " " "A" " " " " " "C" "
"D" Coy. will detail 1 L.G. & team to report to "B" Coy.

2. The 13th Yorkshire Regt. will take over billets as under:-
"C" Coy. Yorks relieve "D" Coy. Suffolks
"B" " " " "A" " "
"D" " " " "C" " "
"A" " " " "B" " "

3. Advance Parties of 1 Officer, 1 N.C.O. & 8 O.R. per Coy. and Bn. Hd. Qrs. will report to 13th Yorkshire Regt. at 6 p.m. to take over stores etc.
Advance Parties of 13th Yorkshire Regt. will assist during the day.

4. Trench Stores will be handed & taken over carefully and signed lists sent to Orderly Room by 9 a.m. 5th inst.

5. Completion of Relief will be wired to Bn. Hd. Qrs. in usual order.

5. The Quarter Master will arrange for:-
   (1) 1 Limber G.S. per Coy
       1 Limber for Bn. Hd. Qrs.,
       Mahlous Cart for Medical Officer,
       to report to Bryer x Hd. Qrs at 8.45 p.m. 4th inst.
   (2) The Water Cart at Bn. Hd. Qrs. to be taken back
       to Tanyboy and the Water Cart at present with
       'J' Coy. to be taken to KITCHEN CRATER.
   (3) Rations to be drawn at usual hour 5pm.

                                    A W Lee
                                    Captain
                                    Adjutant,
                                    12th Bn. Suffolk Regiment.

Appendix I.   War Diary.

Operation Orders
by
Major G. Clarke
Commanding 1/4th Suffolk Regt.

Sept 12th 1917.

The Battalion will be relieved by the Yorkshire Regt. on night of 12/13th. Sept. as under:-

Yorkshire Regt.   Suffolk Regt.
"D" Company will relieve "D" Company
"A"   "   "   "A"   "
"B"   "   "   "B"   "
"C"   "   "   "C"   "

Company H.Qrs. will march to Bruay. Billets are allotted as under:-

"A" Company   VAUCELETTE FARM.
"B"   "   HEUDECOURT.
"C"   "   "   Y roads
"D"   "   "   Sysaem.
Snipers   VAUCELETTE FARM   Souscorps Crock
Bn. H.Q. Ors. HEUDICOURT.
               VAUCELETTE FARM.

Guides. None required.
Advance parties of 1 Officer + 1 NCO per Coy + Bn H.Q. Ors. will report to the Yorkshire Regt. to which one Coys do. at 5 p.m.

At arrival parties of Bn. Yorkshire Regt. will arrive during the day. Local Guides will be carefully detailed and meet the Platoons at Vaucel. Farm by guides. Wh. inst.

Companies of relief will be armed in usual state. O.O. type will also inform Bn.H.Qrs when they have arrived in their respective positions in trenches.

Coys left at HEUDECOURT are allotted as under on 13th inst:-

"B" Company   11 a.m. to   12 noon.
"C" Company   12 noon   12.30 p.m.
"D" Company   2 p.m.   2.30 p.m.
"A" Company   2.30 p.m.   3.30 p.m.
Details   3.30 p.m.   4.30 p.m.
               4.30 p.m.   5.0 p.m.

All Headquarters and Snipers will attend with their Coys.
Transport Officer will arrange:-
(1) To send Officers orderlies to respective Coys.
(2) 1 limber per coy. and Headquarters, 2 wtr carts & 2 mess carts to report to respective Coys every day for carriage of water of the sort.

A.W. Cave Captain
           Adjutant
1/4 Bn. Suffolk Regiment.

Appendix 3
Copy No. 12.

Battalion Orders
by
Lieut Col J Earsley Wilmot DSO
Commdg 12th Bn Suffolk Regt.

Sept 16th 1917

1. The Battalion will relieve 20th Middlesex Regt in Support west of Hillside Dept as under:-

   Suffolks   Middlesex
   "A" Bty   relieve   "A" Bty   in CEMETERY Road.
   "B"   "   "   "B" "   in Reserve Line
   "C"   "   "   "C" "   in CEMETERY Road.
   "D"   "   "   "D" "   in GONNELIEU WOOD

   Suffolks will remain in their present billets until dark. Middlesex
   2nd Middlesex will take over as under:-

   Middlesex   Suffolks
   "A" Bty take over from   "A" Bty
   "B"   "   "   "   "B"   "
   "C"   "   "   "   "C"   "
   "D"   "   "   "   "D"   "

2. Guides   NIL

3. Advance Party of 1 Officer & 1 N.C.O. per Bty & Bn. H.Qrs will report to 2nd Middlesex at 4 pm & take over stores.

4. Battalion Guides for 2nd Middlesex will arrive during the forenoon.

5. Principal Officers will arrange
   (a) so that Officer's kits by 5 pm.
   (b) to send Limber for "A" Bty & B.H.Q. at 5-30 pm.
   Limbers: Middlesex last to Bn.H.Q. by 7pm.
   1 Limber "A" Middlesex kits to B.H.Q. by 9 pm. 11-15 pm.

6. Completion of relief will be sent to Brigade Room by 9 pm. 11-15 pm.
   Completion of relief will be sent to Bn.H.Q. in record time i.e. none of Bty.
   Commanders

   (Sgd) A W Little Captain & Adjutant
                    12th Bn Suffolk Regiment.

   Copies: 1. B.2.Bty   7. Quarter Master
            2. B.3."   8. Signal Officer
            3. B.C."   9. Medical Officer
            4. B.D."   10. B.S.M.
            5. Transport   11. War Diary
            6. Intelligence Officer 12.

Officers personally responsible that Billets are left clean.

Appendix of War Diary

Operation Orders
by
Lieut Col. J. Elvidge-Wilmot, D.S.O.
Comdg. 12th Bn. Suffolk Regt.

Sept 18th 1917.

The Battalion will be relieved by 21st Middlesex Regt on night of 19/20th Sept.
On relief the Battalion will move to Reserve quarters taking over from 20th Middlesex
"C" Coy. will take over Huts VAUCELETTE.
"D"   "   "   "   "   "   Metairie, MEDUCOURT.
"A"   "   "   "   "   "   Square
"B"   "   "   "   "   "   Sunkenroad, VAUCELETTE
H.Q. "   "   "   "   "   VAUCELETTE FARM

The 21st Middlesex will take over as under:-
Middlesex.   Suffolks.
"A" Coy.   relieve   "C" Coy.
"B"   "   "   "D" "
"C"   "   "   "A" "
"D"   "   "   "B" "

Advance Parties of 21st Middlesex will arrive during the day.
The Transport Officer with the Coy. Cooks &
(1) Latrine Sergt by Decauville return limber
     Limber & Mules & Cart to Bn. Rd. Hd.
(2) To deliver rations cooked ready for next day's rations.
Trench Stores will be handed over to relieving person
by 2 o'clock 20th instant.
Coys. platoons of relief and reserve in reserve will be reported to relieving person by usual route.

(Sgd) A. M. West Captain
                    Adjutant
                12th Bn. Suffolk Regt.

Appendix S

Operation Orders
by
Lieut. Col. T.E.A. Radley-Walters DSO
Commanding 12th Bn. Suffolk Regt.

Sept 23rd 1917

The Battalion will relieve the 12th Yorkshire Regt. in Left Sub-Sector on night of 23rd-24th Sept. as under:-

Suffolks   Yorks
D Coy. relieve   Right Front Coy.
A "   "   Left Front Coy.
B "   "   Right Support and Reserve
C "   "   Left Support.

Snipers   Snipers
&
Scouts   Scouts

2. D & A Coys. will march via Sulva & Station in Battalion order & relieve in the Support lines. On arrival they are also to relieve the Yorks of Z & Y Coys. will be unable to B Coy. will leave Sulva Farm about 6am, for B.H.Q.

3. B Coy. will guide the Lewis and other guns for D Coy. with string, etc. to the trenches.

4. Advance Parties will report to Guides in support lines at 6 pm. The rear parties will take over stores, etc.

5. 12th Bn. Suffolks Regt. will move to Bourrie alongside of platoons to take over stores, etc.

6. French Stove Lists will be sent to C.O. as soon as possible in the forms issued for same.

7. Casualties of all kinds will be reported to B.H.Q. as received there.

8. The number of H.E. & Stokes mortar shells expended will come into use at once.

9. The Lewis gun Officer will arrange for:-
   (a) Reports daily to the batteries by 2 30 pm
   (b) Lewis gun boxes are to be filled with S.A.A. and kept at Cy position
   (c) 1 complete Lewis gun limber for supplies to Battalion to be delivered at once from S.A.A.

       AliCan
       Captain
       12th Bn. Suffolk Regiment.

S E C R E T.
Copy No. ....

OPERATION ORDERS

by

Lieutenant-Colonel T. Eardley-Wilmot, D. S. O.,

Commanding 1st. Bn. Suffolk Regiment.

21st September, 1917.

Ref. Special Sheet Ed. 1,
GOUZEAUCOURT 1/20,000.

1. Raid will be carried out on night 25th/26th September on enemy's trenches in R.28.d.

2. Objects.

   (i). Obtain prisoners, identifications and material.
   (ii). Destroy dug-outs, material and defences.

3. ZERO hour will be notified later.
   Parties will be in position about 50 yds N.E. of NEWTON ROAD and facing the enemy trenches 5 minutes before Zero.

4. Raid will be carried out under a creeping barrage. During the day a bombardment of the enemy trenches by Artillery and Trench Mortars will take place. A gap in enemy's wire will be cut about R.26.c.10.95.
   Detail and action of Raiding Parties on separate sheets.

5. At Zero a 3 minutes barrage will fall on the front line and will creep at 25 yards per minute to R.28.d.00.50. - R.28.d.85.50. It will remain on that for 5 minutes. At end of 5 minutes it will creep forward at the same rate to R.28.d.10.75. - R.28.d.65.75., and will remain on that line for 3 minutes. At the end of 3 minutes it will creep forward over enemy's trenches and establish a box barrage. Box Barrage remains until Zero + 70 minutes, by which time all parties will be clear of enemy trenches.

6. Signal for withdrawal will be a series of short whistle blasts.
   All ranks to be warned that the word "RETIRE" will not be used. If orders are necessary, the word "WITHDRAW" will be used.
   O.C. Parties will be responsible for the withdrawal of their men.

7. No identifications, letters or maps will be carried.
   All ranks will be issued with a number, to be worn on left wrist.

8. All wounded and prisoners to be evacuated at once. Prisoners to Advanced Battalion Headquarters, together with any identifications. Advanced Battalion Headquarters will be in CHESHIRE QUARRY. Advanced Dressing Station will be in CHESHIRE QUARRY. Medical Officer will make necessary arrangements for evacuation of wounded.

- 2 -

9. Signalling Officer will arrange the following :-
   (a). Advanced Runner and Telephone Post at head of BICESTER AVENUE R.34.b.00.45. to connect with Battalion Headquarters.
   (b). A Telephone to go with Raiding Party.

10. Battle Police will be established at :-

    TURNER'S QUARRY.
    Top of BROADHURST AVENUE.
    Top of BICESTER AVENUE.
    Top of WILLIS AVENUE.
    Top of HUSH ALLEY.

11. Identifications :-

    Runners   - RED   band. }
    Moppers up   - WHITE band. } bands to be worn round
    Signallers   - BLUE band. } the left forearm.
    Salvage   - KHAKI band.

12. Watches to be synchronised.
    All Officers to have compasses and know bearings to their objective and way back.
    All ranks should be warned to note the direction of the wind, if any, or moon, so that they do not lose their way.

13. As casualties may occur, understudies for all Commands will be told off.
    Each man will know exactly what he is to do and where/is to go.

14. Raiders will return by any route, wherever the enemy's barrage can best be avoided. Parties will report to Advanced Officers and N.C.O's i/c. Other ranks will proceed Battalion Headquarters on their return. straight to billets where they will hand in their disses.

F. Earley Petrush
Lieutenant-Colonel,
Commanding 12th Battalion Suffolk Regiment.

Copy No 1. to M.I. By 1st Sec
      2.
      3.   OC A Coy
      4.   OC B Coy
      5.   Group I/C Coy
      6.   NHP
      7.   Her Maj.
      8.   OC 12 M.G.C
      9.   War Diary

No. 1 PARTY.

Composition.

2 officers, 52 other ranks, 1 Lewis Gun. - divided as follows :-

- (a). Main Party   1 officer, 22 other ranks.
- (b). Blocking Party   1 N.C.O., 7 other ranks, 1 Lewis Gun.
- (c). Moppers up   1 officer, 14 other ranks, 6 R.E's,
                           4 Salvage men, 4 Stretcher Bearers.

Equipment.

(a). Main Party. Rifle and bayonet, 20 rounds per man, 4 bombs (Mills No. 5).
Among Party. 2 electric torches, 4 doz. bombs (Mills No. 5), 2 doz. Grenados (Mills No.23), 4 bomb cups, 12 hand wire cutters with lanyard.

(b). Blocking Party. Rifle and bayonet, 20 rounds per man (Nos. 1 & 2 L.G. revolver and 20 rounds), 4 bombs per man.
Among Party. 1 L.G. WITH medium sights, 4 magazines, 6 barbed wire Gooseberries, 1 electric torch, 2 doz. bombs (Mills No. 5).

(c). Moppers up. Rifle and bayonet, except Salvage men and Stretcher Bearers, 20 rounds, 4 bombs per man, 2 electric torches, 2 doz. Mills No. 5, 1 doz. 'P' bombs, mobile charges, 2 stretchers.

A C T I O N.

(a). Main Party.

Follow close up behind barrage, strike enemy trench at R.28.d.65.30. and proceed along Right Boyeau on each side of trench to BLEAK SUPPORT, thence along latter to R.29.d.35.95.

(b). Blocking Party.

Follow close behind Main Party to BLEAK SUPPORT, then turn Eastwards and block BLEAK SUPPORT 50 yds from junction. Lewis Gun to be in position on parados facing N.E. with proper field of fire.

(c). Moppers up.

Follow close behind Main Party, jump into trench at R.28.d.65.30. and move along Right Boyeau and then along BLEAK SUPPORT keeping level with Main Party, and dropping men from rear at each dug-out, one man and one R.E. at each entrance to dug-outs.
Salvage men collect all moveable material and take back to local support.
Stretcher Bearers take back any wounded men to supports.
O.C. Moppers up will detail men to escort back any prisoners to supports.

No. 2 PARTY.

Composition.

1 Officer, 29 Other ranks - divided as follows :-

(a). **Main Party.** 1 Officer, 15 Other ranks.

(b). **Hoppers up.** 1 N.C.O., 9 Other ranks, 2 R.E's, 2 Stretcher Bearers.

Equipment.

(a). **Main Party.** Rifle and bayonet, 20 rounds, 4 bombs per man.
Among Party.
1 electric torch, 2 doz. Mills No. 5, 1 doz. Mills No. 23, 2 bomb cups, 10 wire cutters.

(b). **Hoppers up.** Rifle and bayonet, 20 rounds, 4 bombs per man.
Among Party.
1 doz. "P" bombs, 2 electric torches, 1 mobile charge, 1 Stretcher.

A C T I O N.

(a). **Main Party.**
Advance close behind barrage in extended order, cross SAP Trench to ELLIS Trench at R.28.d.40.45. Thence a small party moves forward keeping touch with flanks and clearing up all shell holes.

(b). **Hoppers up.**
Follow close behind Main Party, drop 4 Other ranks in SAP Trench to work along same to Right Boyeau. Remainder with R.E's and Stretcher Bearers enter ELLIS Trench and work along same to Right Boyeau.

No. 3 PARTY.   SUPPORTS.

Composition.

1 Officer, 24 Other ranks, 1 Lewis Gun.

Equipment. ...   Rifle and bayonet, 30 rounds, 4 bombs
                  per man.
                  Among Party.
                  1 Lewis Gun, 6 magazines, 2 electric
                  torches, 4 doz. Mills No. 5, 2 doz.
                  Mills No. 23, 6 'P' bombs, 2 Stretchers,
                  4 bomb cups, 6 hand wire cutters, 6
                  barbed wire gooseberries.

A C T I O N.

Advance just to rear and right flank of No. 1 Party, and establish H.Q. in SAP Trench about R.28.d.70.30.
Detail party to block SAP Trench to the East.
Be prepared to reinforce Blocking Party of No. 1 Party if any attack develops there.
Lewis Gun to be in position to cover right flank and whole party to be ready to meet any attack from the Right.

No. 4 PARTY.

Composition.

1 Officer, 29 Other ranks - divided as follows :-

(a). **Main Party.**   1 Officer, 15 Other ranks.
(b). **Moppers up.**   1 N.C.O., 9 Other ranks, 2 R.E's, 2 Stretcher Bearers.

Equipment.

Same as No. 2 Party.

A C T I O N.

(a). **Main Party.**

Advance close behind barrage in extended order, cross SAP Trench to BEER Trench at R.20.d.20.40. Thence a small party moves forward clearing up ground to R.28.d.35.90. and keeping touch with parties on their flanks.

(b). **Moppers up.**

Follow behind Main Party, drop 4 in SAP Trench to work to left, remainder in Centre Boyau to work up to BEER TRENCH and then a long to left (Westwards) to No. 5 Party.

No. 5 PARTY.

Composition.

2 Officers, 40 Other ranks - divided as follows :-

(a). Main Party. 1 Officers, 20 Other ranks.
(b). Moppers up. 1 Officer, 16 Other ranks, 6 R.E's,
                  2 Stretcher Bearers, 4 Salvage men.

Equipment.

(a). Main Party.   Rifle and bayonet, 20 rounds, 4 bombs per man.
                    Among Party.
                    2 electric torches, 12 hand wire cutters
                    4 doz. bombs Mills No. 5, 2 doz.
                    Grenades Mills No. 23, 4 bomb cups.

(b). Moppers up.   Rifle and bayonet, 20 rounds, 4 bombs per man.
                    Among Party.
                    3 electric torches, 2 doz. bombs Mills
                    No. 5, 1 doz. 'P' bombs, mobile
                    charges, 1 Stretcher.

A C T I O N.

(a). Main Party.

Advance behind barrage with left flank on CHESHIRE STREET to SEA Trench, thence along road to BLEAK SUPPORT.

(b). Moppers up.

Drop men at all dug-outs on road between BEER Trench and SEA Trench, clear up trench and any other dug-outs. Escorts for prisoners to be provided and prisoners sent back to supports. Salvage men collect and bring back material.

No. 6 PARTY.   SUPPORTS.

Composition.

1 Officer, 24 Other ranks, 3 Signallers.

Equipment.

Same as No. 3 Party, including Lewis Gun.

A C T I O N.

H.Q. Advance on left rear flank of No. 5 Party and establish near CHESHIRE STREET in BEER TRENCH.
Detail party to block EIR Trench West of Road.
Lewis Gun to take up position to cover left forward flank.
Signallers to get into telephonic communication with Battalion Headquarters.

APPENDIX A

On night of 26th September 6C raided the enemy trenches in R.28.d. after heavy Artillery bombardment. The enemy sent out our party forming up in No-mans land & this bombing came down 9 minutes before our causing considerable casualties. Our raiding party advanced & was followed across by the enemy barrage. Riflemen reached his trenches & bombers killing many in the trenches & Lewis gunners playing up the entrance of store from which the enemy refused to come out. Out of a total of 8 officers & 236 OR our casualties were 1 Officer Capt MEH SCHIFF wounded & various + officers 2/Lts R.T. ROBINS. G. HALLSMITH J.T. SUTTLE J. FLYETT + 92 OR

Appendix B

Following wires received with reference to Raid carried out 27.6. Sept

"Following from G.O.C. Division begins aaa Please convey to 1st Suffolks my appreciation of this very gallant effort to obtain identification. The enemy effort a very heavy fire which the Batt. came under, that Spirit their objective, inflicted severe losses on the enemy & brought back prisoners aaa I much regret to hear that the Batt. suffered some casualties in carrying out the attack aaa Ends aaa"

"Following from Division begins aaa Please convey to B 12 x 15 Suffolks the congratulations of the Corps Commander on their success & on the fine spirit shown by all ranks during the Raid aaa Ends aaa"

"Following from Div: begins aaa Wire from Corps aaa Wire from General O.I.N.G. Army Commander begins aaa Convey my hearty congratulations to 12 Suffolk on their successful raid"

To be made up to and for Sunday in each week.

No. of Report_____

FIELD RETURN.

Army Form B. 213.

(To be furnished by all arms, services, and departments (except A.S.C. units) to the A. G.'s Office at the Base in accordance with Field Service Regulations, Part II.)

RETURN showing numbers   (a) Effective strength of Unit.   _____ at _____ _____ Date.
(b) Rationed by Unit.

DETAIL	Personnel			Animals.								Guns, carriages, and limbers and transport vehicles												Motor Bicycles	Bicycles	REMARKS
				Horses				Mules				Guns, carriages and limbers, showing description	Ammunition wagons and limbers	Machine guns	Aircraft, showing description	Horsed		Mechanical								
	Officers	Other ranks	Natives	Riding	Draught	Heavy Draught	Pack	Large	Small	Camels	Oxen					4 wheeled	2 wheeled	Motor Cars.	Tractors	Lorries, showing description	Trucks, showing description	Trailers				
Effective Strength of Unit																										
Details, *by Arms* attached to unit as in War Establishment :—																										
Total																										
War Establishment																										
Wanting to complete (Detail of Personnel and Horses below)																										
Surplus																										
*Attached (not to include the details shown above)																										
Civilians :— Employed with the Unit Accompanying the Unit																										
TOTAL RATIONED...																										

* In the case of field ambulances, hospitals or depots, the number of patients are to be included here, the names being shown in A. F. A. 36.

_____ Signature of Commander.

_____ Date of Despatch.

Army Form B. 213.

FIELD RETURN

To be made up to and for Sunday in each week.

For information of the A.G.'s Office at the Base.

Officers and men who have become casuals, been transferred or joined since last report.

Place _____ Date _____

Regtl. Number	Rank	Name	Corps	Nature of casualty or name of unit from or to which transferred	Date of being struck off or coming on the ration return	Remarks*

Signature of Commander _____

Date of despatch _____

* State whether absence is of a permanent or temporary nature, adding, in the case of casuals from wounds or disease, any available information for communication to the relatives.

Only additional information regarding "wanting to complete," and sufficient information to explain the difference between the present and previous week's effective strength is to be entered on this side.

WAR DIARY
1st Bn SUFFOLK REGT
From 1/10/17 To 31/10/17
(Volume 17)

Original

Demands made on this sheet should consist of personnel required from the Base only, and should not include any demands for personnel which can be completed by promotions or appointments within the unit.

Perforated Sheet giving detail of personnel and horses wanting to complete, shown on Army Form B. 213.

No. of Report _____

Detail of Wanting to Complete.	Drivers						Gunners	Smith Gunners	Range Takers	Farriers		Shoeing and Carriage Smiths	Cold Shoers	Wheelers			Saddlers or Harness Makers	Blacksmiths	Bricklayers and Masons	Carpenters and Joiners	Fitters & Turners (R.E.)		Fitters		Plumbers	Electricians		Signalmen	Engine Drivers		Air Line Men	Permanent Line Men	Operators, Telegraph	Cablemen	Brigade Section Pioneers	General-duty Pioneers	Signallers	Instrument Repairers	Motor Cyclist	Motor Cyclist Artificers	Telephonists	Clerks	Machine Gunners	Armament Artificers		Armourers	Storemen	Privates	W.O's and N.C.O's (by ranks) not included in trade columns					TOTAL to agree with wanting to complete		Horses			
	R.A.	R.E.	A.S.C.	Car	Lorry	Steam				Serjeants	Corporals			R.A.	H.T.	M.T.					Wood	Iron	R.A.	Wireless		Ordinary	W.T.		Loco.	Field														Fitters	Range Finders										Officers	Other Ranks	Riding	Draught	Heavy Draught	Pack
CAVALRY																																																											
R.A.																																																										
R.E.																																																										
INFANTRY																																																										
R.A.M.C.																																																										
A.O.C.																																																										
A.V.C.																																																										

Remarks :—

_____ Signature of Commander.

_____ Unit.

_____ Formation to which attached.

_____ Date of Despatch.

(6305) Wt. W2927/M2226. 1,250,000. 6/17. McA. & W., Ltd. (E1348). Forms B2138/8. [P.T.O.

WAR DIARY
or
INTELLIGENCE SUMMARY

Army Form C. 2118.

Sept. 17th/18th September 1917

Place	Date	Hour	Summary of Events and Information	Remarks and references to Appendices
GOUZEAUCOURT			October 1917	
	1		In trenches. Quiet. Relieved by 13th YORKSHIRE Reg.t & moved	
			to Support Camp	
	2		In Support Camp	
	3		" " "	
	4		" " "	
	5		" Relieved by 1/21st MIDDLESEX & moved to reserve camp	
	6		In reserve "	
VAUCELETTE FARM	7		" " "	
	8		" " "	
	9		Moved to SOREL. Relieved by 12th KINGS LIVERPOOLS Camp	
SOREL	10		Moved by bus to PERONNE Camp	
PERONNE	11		Moved by rail at 10 pm to BEAUMETZ Stn & marched to	
			RAVINCOURT Camp	
RAVINCOURT	12		At FILLE in RAVINCOURT Camp	
MARSTC	13		" " " " Camp	
	14.7.58		" " " " Camp	

Sheet II   **WAR DIARY** *12 Bn Suffolk Regt*   Army Form C. 2118
or
INTELLIGENCE SUMMARY.
(Erase heading not required.)

Place	Date	Hour	Summary of Events and Information	Remarks and references to Appendices
	October			
RAVINCOURT	29		Moved to billets in SUS-ST-LEGER area	
MAP 51C	30-31		In billets in SUS ST LEGER area	
			Strength on Oct 1 — 39 Officers — 882 O.R.	
			" " " 31 — 40 " — 990 O.R.	
			Casualties during the month — NIL.	
			Reinforcements " " " — 2/Lt F. NADAL	
			" G. HALLSMITH	
			111. O.R.	
			The following decorations were awarded for Gallant Conduct on the night 25/26 September.	
			Capt H.A. REDDING Bar to M.C. № 14457 C.S.M. MORLEY G.N. Military Medal	
			2/Lt R.T. ROBINS " 21550 Sgt BODLE. G " "
			" H. WILLIAMS M.C. 22154 L/Cpl MARSHALL A.F " "
			21343 " LANGLEY. F " "
			8131 Sgt BLINCO. C D.C.M. 34857 Pte MUTIMER. R " "
			27449 " McMAHON " 35110 " WOODROW C.E " "
			15811 Pte PRATT "	
			F. Rawley Wilaud Lt Col	
			Comdg 12 Bn Suffolk Regt	

To be made up to and for Saturday in each week

No. of Report _____

FIELD RETURN.

Army Form B. 213

(To be furnished by all arms, services, and departments (except A.S.C. units) to the A.G.'s Office at the Base in accordance with Field Service Regulations, Part II.)

RETURN showing numbers (a) Effective strength of Unit.
(b) Rationed by Unit. _____ at _____ _____ Date.

DETAIL	Personnel			Animals						Guns and transport vehicles													REMARKS
				Horses			Mules							Horsed		Mechanical							
	Officers	Other ranks	Natives	Riding	Draught	Heavy Draught	Pack	Large	Small	Guns, showing description	Ammunition wagons	Machine guns	Aircraft, showing description	4 Wheeled	2 Wheeled	Motor Cars	Tractors	Lorries, showing description	Trucks, showing description	Trailers	Motor Bicycles	Bicycles	Motor Ambulances	
Effective Strength of Unit......																								
Details *by Arms* attached to unit as in War Establishment:—																								
Total																								
War Establishment																								
Wanting to complete (Detail of Personnel and Horses below)																								
Surplus																								
*Attached (not to include the details shown above)........																								
Civilians:— Employed with the Unit......																								
Accompanying the Unit......																								
TOTAL RATIONED......																								

* In the case of field ambulances, hospitals or depots, the number of patients are to be included here, the names being shown in A.F.A. 36.

_____ Signature of Commander. _____ Date of Despatch.

FIELD RETURN

For information of the A.G.'s Office at the base.

Officers and men who have become casuals, been transferred or joined since last report.

Place _____

Regtl. Number	Rank	Name	Corps	Date	Nature of casualty, or name of unit from or to which transferred	Date of being struck off or coming on the ration return	Remarks*

* State whether absence is of a permanent or temporary nature, adding, in the case of casuals from wounds or disease, any available information for communication to the relatives.

Vol 18
121/40

WAR DIARY
12th SUFFOLK REGT.
from Nov 1st to Nov 30/17
(Volume 18)

Original Rey

[Page is upside down; blank pre-printed British Army form]

[P.T.O.

Date of Despatch _____

Formation to which attached _____

Unit _____

Signature of Commander _____

Remarks :—

Demands made on this sheet should not include any demands for personnel which can be completed by promotions or appointments within the unit.

Perforated Sheet giving detail of personnel and horses waiting to complete, shown on Army Form B. 213.

No. of Report _____

(7422.) Wt. W14775/M1525 1,000,000 2/17 (E834) Forms B213/8 D.&N., London, E.C.

To be made up to and for Saturday in each week

No. of Report _____

FIELD RETURN.

Army Form B 213

(To be furnished by all arms, services, and departments (except A.S.C. units) to the A.G.'s Office at the Base in accordance with Field Service Regulations, Part II.)

RETURN showing numbers (a) Effective strength of Unit. _____ at _____ _____ Date.
(b) Rationed by Unit.

DETAIL	Personnel			Animals						Guns and transport vehicles.													REMARKS
				Horses				Mules				Machine guns		Horsed		Mechanical							
	Officers	Other ranks	Natives	Riding	Draught	Heavy Draught	Pack	Large	Small	Guns, showing description	Ammunition wagons		Aircraft, showing description	4 Wheeled	2 Wheeled	Motor Cars	Tractors	Lorries, showing description	Trucks, showing description	Trailers	Motor Bicycles	Bicycles	Motor Ambulances	
Effective Strength of Unit......																								
Details *by Arms* attached to unit as in War Establishment :—																								
Total																								
War Establishment																								
Wanting to complete (Detail of Personnel and Horses below)																								
Surplus																								
Attached (not to include the details shown above)............																								
Civilians :— Employed with the Unit																								
Accompanying the Unit																								
TOTAL RATIONED......																								

* In the case of field ambulances, hospitals or depots, the number of patients are to be included here, the names being shown in A.F.A. 36.

_____ Signature of Commander. _____ Date of Despatch.

For information of the A.G.'s Office at the base.

Officers and men who have become casuals, been transferred or joined since last report.

Place _____   Date _____

Regtl. Number	Rank	Name	Corps	Nature of casualty, or name of unit from or to which transferred	Date of being struck off or coming on the ration return	Remarks*

*State whether absence is of a permanent or temporary nature, adding, in the case of casuals from wounds or disease, any available information for communication to the relatives.

Sheet 1 WAR DIARY or INTELLIGENCE SUMMARY 13th B" Suffolk Regt Army Form C. 2118.

(Erase heading not required.)

Place	Date	Hour	Summary of Events and Information	Remarks and references to Appendices
	1917 November			
SUS ST LEGER	1st to 16th		Training in SUS ST LEGER. Moved on 16th to billets in BAVINCOURT. AWC	
BAVINCOURT	16		In billets AWC	
	17		Moved to ACHIET LE PETIT at night AWC	
ACHIET LE PETIT	18		In Camp AWC	
"	19		Moved to ROCQUIGNY at night AWC	
ROCQUIGNY	20		Resting in huts at ROCQUIGNY AWC	
"	21		Moved to BEAUMETZ LEZ CAMBRAI AWC	
BEAUMETZ LEZ CAMBRAI	22		In Camp at BEAUMETZ. Moved to trenches in BOURLON. Relieved 63rd Div as Reserve Batt. in Road E 29 c and d. Map 57C SE	
BOURLON	23		The 13th Yorkshire & 20th Middlesex Regts attacked enemy position in front of BOURLON. 13th SUFFOLKS in Reserve. After attack we advanced to position vacated by 21 MIDDX. 4 Coys in trench in E 29 a. Bn. H.Qrs. E 29 a. 6.3.	
	23	12 noon	"B" Coy reinforced 20 MIDDX. "C" Coy reported to 21st MIDDX. "D" Coy proceeded to E 23 C	

Sheet II   WAR DIARY   12ᵗʰ Bⁿ Suffolk Regt   Army Form C. 2118.

or

INTELLIGENCE SUMMARY.

(Erase heading not required.)

Instructions regarding War Diaries and Intelligence Summaries are contained in F. S. Regs., Part II. and the Staff Manual respectively. Title pages will be prepared in manuscript.

Place	Date	Hour	Summary of Events and Information	Remarks and references to Appendices
BOULLON	23	3 noon	outside the Beet factory on the CAMBRAI ROAD	
			"A" Coy in trenches E 29 a. AWG	
"		4pm	Position of Batt. 1 Coy in trenches E 29 a 1 Coy in Shell holes E 33 a + b 1 Coy in front line E 13 c. 2 Platoon in front line E 13 c. + E 19 d. 2 Platoon in Road E 23 b. & 8. Bⁿ H Q. E 29 a 6. 3.	
			Brigade Hd Qrs reported in position for attack behind Bⁿ H Q.	
			In the evening at a Conference held at Hd Qrs 20ᵗʰ MIDDX arrangements were made for the Cavalry to take over the left of line + the Coy in Shell holes in E 33 a + b to retire to Beet factory + cover it at E 23 b. AWG	
"	24	4 am	Orders received that Counter attack was probable. Arranged details with O C Coy to meet it	
"		6 am	Bⁿ in position as follows. B + D Coy in front line under orders of O C 20 MIDDX C Coy in Shell holes in E 33 a + b. A Coy in reserve in E 29 a. Bⁿ H Q E 29 a	
"		10 am	Vickers Guns retired from front line in E 33 a. 1 Platoon C Coy + 2 Lewis Guns sent forward to take their place.	
			Received orders to attack BOULLON VILLAGE Issued orders for attack	

T2134. Wt. W708—776. 500000. 4/15. Sir J. C. & S.

Sheet III   WAR DIARY   13th Bn Suffolk Regt
or
INTELLIGENCE SUMMARY.
(Erase heading not required.)

Army Form C. 2118.

Place	Date	Hour	Summary of Events and Information	Remarks and references to Appendices
Boursies	24		B on right D on left A in Support C in Reserve. Withdrew 2 platoons C Coy from front line	
"	"	12 noon	Coys in position for attack. Bn HQ moved to Quarry E 24 c	
"	"	3 pm	Attack launched B Coy penetrated the village on the right D Coy held up by M.G. fire A Coy moved to reinforce D Coy. C Coy reinforced B Coy	
"	"	5 pm	News received that Batt on right were digging in in Wood at E12 d 63. + issued orders for Coy to return to old line. After all Coys had withdrawn positions were taken up as under. 1 Coy 20th MIDDX right front. 2 " 13th SUFFOLKS left front 1 " " " Reserve in Sunken Rd E17 d. 1 " " " Support E 18.6.	
"	"	7 pm	East Surrey Regt + 2 Coy King's Own reported. The King's Own were sent to Reserve. 2 Coy 20th MIDDX withdrawn. AWG	
"	25th		No change. Heavy shelling. Relieved by York + Lancaster Regt 62nd Div + moved to trenches in Hindenburg Support line. AWG	

WAR DIARY or INTELLIGENCE SUMMARY

Army Form C. 2118.

Sheet IV   13 September

Place	Date	Hour	Summary of Events and Information	Remarks and references to Appendices
Hindenburg Line	26		Fired A BAVINCOURT aug	
BAVINCOURT	27	1 am	Marched to YPRES + entrained for BERTMETZ. Aune + then marched to BAILLEULMONT.	
			F Batty " BAILLEULMONT Arey KENS 11 aug	
BAILLEULMONT	28		Jn Billet aug	
	29	"	aug	
	30	"	aug	

Casualties. Wounded A/Lt Robinson A/S G Miller. KEITHYMARK FT VERRY

J FRYETT   OR 97

A/Lt R PEARCE   Severely Wounded   OR 3
A/Lt C HALLSMITH Remained at duty   OR 4

                              Killed   OR 26
                              Missing   OR 6
                      Wounded believed killed OR 7

Strength Nov 1st   40 Officers   990 OR
"   " 30th   37 Officers   825 OR

Reinforcement during the month. Capt A PROCTER 2/Lt C CRUDAS 2/Lt WHITING

T134. W1. W708-776. 500000. 4/15. Sir J.C.&S.   O.F. 16.

Postponedash aug

T.R.

WAR DIARY or ~~INTELLIGENCE SUMMARY~~

Sheet I   12th Bn Suffolk Regt   Army Form C. 2118.

(Erase heading not required.)

Place	Date	Hour	Summary of Events and Information	Remarks and references to Appendices
LENS II	December			
BAILLEUMONT	1		Moved by route march to Camp at HAMELINCOURT AMC	
HAMELINCOURT	2		Took over front line in TUNNEL TRENCH from 16th Division. 17th Welch on right 21st Middx on left AMC	
TUNNEL TRENCH U.7.d.k. V.1.r.a.	3		Quiet AMC	
	4		Quiet. AMC	
	5		Our Artillery active enemy quiet AMC	
	6		" " " " " AMC	
	7		" " " " " AMC	
	8		" " " " " AMC	
	9		" " " " " AMC	
	10		Relieved by 14th ARGYLE & SUTHERLANDS & marched to HAMELINCOURT in Camp AMC	
HAMELINCOURT	11		In Camp. "Stood to" at 6.30am AMC	
	12		" " "Stood to" at 6.30 am Moved to 2nd line of defence at 6.55 am & returned to Camp at 10 am AMC	
	13		Moved to Second line of Defence at 4 am Returned to Camp at 9 am AMC	

| | | WAR DIARY or INTELLIGENCE SUMMARY. | | Army Form C. 2118. |

Sheet II   12th Bn Suffolk Regt

Instructions regarding War Diaries and Intelligence Summaries are contained in F. S. Regs., Part II. and the Staff Manual respectively. Title pages will be prepared in manuscript.

(Erase heading not required.)

Place	Date	Hour	Summary of Events and Information	Remarks and references to Appendices
HAMELINCOURT	14		Moved to Second line of Defence at 4.30 am Returned to Camp at 8 am AWC.	
"	15		Stood to at 6.30 am. No action followed Remained in Camp AWC	
"	16		Stood to at 6.30 am No action followed Remained in Camp AWC	
"	17		Remained in Camp AWC	
CROISILLES	18		Relieved 14th ARGYLE & SUTHERLAND HIGHLANDERS as Right Support Batt. Bn Hd Qrs at T 23. C 7. 9. Slight enemy shelling. Our Artillery very active AWC	
"	19		Some Shelling AWC	
"	20		Quiet Slight Shelling on both side AWC	
"	21		Quiet day AWC	
"	22		Some Shelling AWC	
"	23		Some shelling AWC	
"	24		Relieved by 14th H.L.I. & marched back to CLONMEL CAMP AWC	
HAMELINCOURT	25		In Camp AWC	
"	26.		" " AWC	
"	27		Relieved the 8th K.O.R.L. in BULLECOURT Right Sub section AWC	

T2134. Wt. W708—776. 500000. 4/15. Sir J. C. & S.

WAR DIARY or INTELLIGENCE SUMMARY. — Sheet III — 12th Bn Suffolk Regt — Army Form C. 2118.

Place	Date	Hour	Summary of Events and Information	Remarks and references to Appendices
			December 1917	
BULLECOURT	28		Some Shelling. 2/Lt F.W. LEEMAN wounded on Patrol	A.W.C
"	29		Usual shelling during day slightly increased towards night	A.W.C
"	30		Lt. B. PLEDGER wounded at 3 a.m. Shelling increased during the day. Heavy shelling all night	A.W.C
"	31		Relieved by 13th Yorkshire Regt & moved to Support in ECOUST	A.W.C
			Strength on Dec 1st 27 Off. 822 O.R.	
			" " " 31st 40 " 813 O.R.	
			Total Casualties Lt. B.F. PLEDGER, Lt. W. LEEMAN 10. O.R.	
			Total Reinforcements Lt. L.G. ROBERTSON 2/Lts. J. DUNN, R.P. HUGHES, C.J. POSTLETHWAITE	

Lennel Floyd Major.
Comdg 12th Bn Suffolk Regt

SECRET

FILE No. **G.12.**

Sub-Nos. 183-

SUBJECT. Minor Operations.

Sub-head. Enemy Attack on 12 Suff: R, 121 Bde, 40 Div.
on 5 Jan/ 1918.

VI Corps.

Referred to	Date.	Referred to	Date.

Sheet I WAR DIARY 13th Bn Suffolk Regt Army Form C. 2118.
or
INTELLIGENCE SUMMARY.
(Erase heading not required.)

Place	Date	Hour	Summary of Events and Information	Remarks and references to Appendices
MAP LENS 11 ECOUST	January 1918 1		In Support to BULLECOURT Sector AWC	
	2		" " " " " AWC	
	3		" " " " " AWC	
	4		Relieved 13th YORKS in Right Sub Sector BULLECOURT AWC	
BULLECOURT	5	6.30am	Enemy attacked right front & succeeded in gaining possession of about 200x of our line. About 250 men advanced under a heavy bombardment. After repeated counter attacks we finally established our original positions at 6.15 pm. The enemy sustained heavy casualties during the advance from his line & also whilst occupying our front. His left was met with such heavy & accurate Lewis Gun & rifle fire whilst coming through his own wire that those who were not casualties hastily retired AWC	
"	6		During the afternoon the enemy again occupied Gap head on our right front. After reconnoitring arrangements were made for artillery cooperation	
"	7		At 4.30am. We counter attacked with artillery cooperation but were	

WAR DIARY
or
INTELLIGENCE SUMMARY

Army Form C. 2118.

Place	Date	Hour	Summary of Events and Information	Remarks and references to Appendices
BULLECOURT	7		Art obsn & wireless lines. Another Quiet day. Enemy occupied but no signs of being relieved by daylight. Regt Offrs consolidation sufficient. 2nd & 4th MIDDLESEX Regt Coys relieved with OMG	
"	8		Enemy heavy battle posns on front. Enemy fired numerous rounds into our front line. Gas shells. He kept up very little reply. Gunfire & one front line Companies were and kept up at the Coy. Coy Capturing 12 prisoners belonging to 11th BAVARIAN I.R. and Cavalry. Relieved by 13th YORKS — removed to Reserve in MORY OMG	
MORY	9		In Reserve OMG	
"	10		" OMG	
"	11		" OMG	
"	12		Relieved 13th YORKS in front line OMG	13th SURREYS on right 20th MIDDX on left 3 Coys
BULLECOURT	13		Quiet day OMG	
"	14		Trench improved, posting of front covers OMG	

13th Suffolk Regt.

WAR DIARY

Sheet III 12th Bn Suffolk Regt

Army Form C. 2118.

Place	Date	Hour	Summary of Events and Information	Remarks and references to Appendices
	Jan 1918			
BULLECOURT	15		Quiet AWC	
"	16		Quiet. Relieved by 13th YORKs & moved to Support at ECOUST. AWC	
ECOUST	17		In Support Bn HQ shelled with 5.9s AWC	
	18		In Support AWC	
	19		In Support AWC	
	20		In Support. Relieved 13th YORKs in front line AWC	
BULLECOURT	21		In Front Line quiet. AWC	
	22		In Front Line quiet AWC	
	23		In Front Line quiet AWC	
	24		In Front Line quiet. Relieved by 13th Yorkshire Regt. AWC	
MORY	25		In Reserve AWC	
	26		" " AWC	
	27		" " AWC	
	28		" " Relieved 13th Yorks in front line AWC	
BULLECOURT	29		In Front Line Quiet AWC	
"	30		" " " Quiet AWC	

Sheet III   **WAR DIARY**   12th B. Suffolk Reg   Army Form C. 2118.

or

INTELLIGENCE SUMMARY.

(Erase heading not required.)

Instructions regarding War Diaries and Intelligence Summaries are contained in F. S. Regs., Part II. and the Staff Manual respectively. Title pages will be prepared in manuscript.

Place	Date	Hour	Summary of Events and Information	Remarks and references to Appendices
			Jan 1918	
BULLECOURT	31.		In front line. Quiet. AMC.	
			Strength on Jan 1st 40 Officers 813 O.R.	
			" " 31st 38 " 753 "	
			Reinforcements during month 79 O.R. 2/Lts A.A WILLIAMS. C.H. HITCHCOCK.	
			Casualties " " 83 O.R. 2/Lt C.J. POSTLETHWAITE Killed	
			Capt A.M.W PROCTOR 2/Lt R.P HUGHES Wounded.	
			Lt H.C MATHEW 2/Lts J.DUNN. E.H HAMMONDS Wounded at duty	
			The following Officers NCO & men received decorations during the month	
Immediate Awards			D.S.O. Major. L. LLOYD. 2/Lt G HALLSMITH	
			M.C. Capt A.H.M PROCTOR 2/Lt L.H KNOWLES. Lt. H.C MATHEW	
			Second Bar to M.C Capt. H.A REDDING	
			D.C.M. 27697. Sgt. LACEY.C. 27375. Sgt BAKER. E.D 27502 Cpl LARWOOD. A.W. 41537 Pte HUNT	
			M.M. 27511. Sgt ROY KEEP 27701. Sgt HALL. G.H. 27699. Sgt SMART. H. 22284 Sgt FULLER. CA	
			13099. L/Cpl WEBB. S 4164 Pte HATHAWAY. JC	

T2134. Wt. W708—776. 500000. 4/15. Sir J. C. & S.

Sheet V — WAR DIARY or INTELLIGENCE SUMMARY — 12th Bn Suffolk Regt — Army Form C. 2118.

Place	Date	Hour	Summary of Events and Information	Remarks and references to Appendices
	Jan 1918		**New Years Honours**	
			M.C. Capt A.M. CROSS Capt F. MISKIN Lt M.F. RICHARDS	
			Mention Lt Col T. EARDLEY WILMOT. DSO Capt A.V. CRUMP	
			T. Eardley Wilmot Lt Col	

Only additional information regarding "wanting to complete" is to be entered on this side.

WAR DIARY
of
15th BN SUFFOLK REGT
From Jan 1st 1918 to Jan 31st 1918
(Volume 20)
Original Copy

Perforated Sheet giving detail of personnel and horses wanting to complete, shown on Army Form B. 213.

Number of Report _____

Detail of Wanting to Complete	Drivers						Gunners	Smith Gunners	Range Takers	Serjeants	Farriers			Wheelers			Saddlers or Harness Makers	Blacksmiths	Bricklayers and Masons	Carpenters and Joiners	Fitters & Turners (R.E.)			Fitters			Electricians			Engine Drivers		Air Line Men	Permanent Line Men	Operators, Telegraph	Cablemen	Brigade Section Pioneers	General-duty Pioneers	Signallers	Instrument Repairers	Motor Cyclists	Motor Cyclist Artificers	Telephonists	Clerks	Machine Gunners	Armament Artificers		Range Finders	Armourers	Storemen	Privates	W.O's. and N.C.O's. (by ranks) not included in trade columns			TOTAL to agree with wanting to complete		Horses			
	R.A.	R.E.	A.S.C.	Car	Lorry	Steam					Corporals	Shoeing, or Shoeing and Carriage Smiths	Cold Shoers	R.A.	H.T.	M.T.					Wood	Iron	R.A.	Wireless	Plumbers	Ordinary	W.T.	Signalmen	Loco.	Field																Fitters					Officers	Other ranks				Riding	Draught	Heavy Draught	Pack
CAVALRY																																																											
R.A.																																																											
R.E.																																																											
INFANTRY																																																											
R.A.M.C.																																																											
A.O.C.																																																											
A.V.C.																																																											

Remarks :—

_____ Signature of Commander.

_____ Unit.

_____ Formation to which attached.

_____ Date of Despatch.

[P.T.O.

Third Army.

Preliminary Report on Enemy attack on 12th Suffolks (40th Division) on the morning of January 5th.

At 6.10 a.m. the enemy opened a heavy barrage lasting about 20 minutes on the front and support lines of the Battalion Sector. An enemy aeroplane, flying very low, fired into our trenches just before the hostile infantry appeared. At 6.32 a.m. the enemy advanced in force - estimated at 250 - on a front extending from U.22.d.8.5. to U.23.c.3.0. The attack was partially repulsed, the enemy having succeeded in entering our line between U.23.c.05.30. and U.23.d.95.45 including the sap at U.23.c.2.4. A bombing attack was immediately organised but failed to dislodge the enemy. A second attempt at 9.30 a.m. was, however, successful in driving the enemy out of our trenches into the sap, and finally out of the sap. The enemy then counter attacked 3 times from the SUNKEN ROAD and was twice driven back with loss, but the third attempt was successful in regaining the sap. A bombing attack by us at 2 p.m. was driven back and a final and successful counter-attack was made at 5.15 p.m. with Artillery and Stokes Mortar co-operation, and our whole line completely retaken.

Casualties:
	Killed.	Wounded.	Missing.
Officers.	-	2 (at duty)	-
Other Ranks.	4	22	20

Some. The majority of the missing are believed to have been killed.

6th January, 1918.

Lieutenant General.
Commanding VI Corps.

To be made up to and for Sunday in each week.

No. of Report _____   FIELD RETURN.   Army Form B. 213.

(To be furnished by all arms, services, and departments (except A.S.C. units) to the A. G.'s Office at the Base in accordance with Field Service Regulations, Part II.)

RETURN showing numbers (a) Effective strength of Unit.
(b) Rationed by Unit.   _____ at _____ _____ Date.

Detail	Personnel			Animals.								Guns, carriages, and limbers and transport vehicles											Remarks
				Horses			Mules					Guns, carriages and limbers, showing description	Ammunition wagons and limbers	Machine guns	Aircraft, showing description	Horsed		Mechanical					
	Officers	Other ranks	Natives	Riding	Draught	Heavy Draught	Pack	Large	Small	Camels	Oxen					4 wheeled	2 wheeled	Motor Cars.	Tractors	Lorries, showing description	Trucks, showing description	Trailers	Motor Bicycles	Bicycles	
Effective Strength of Unit Details, by *Arms* attached to unit as in War Establishment:—																									
Total																									
War Establishment																									
Wanting to complete (Detail of Personnel and Horses below)																									
Surplus																									
*Attached (not to include the details shown above) Civilians:— Employed with the Unit Accompanying the Unit																									
Total Rationed...																									

* In the case of field ambulances, hospitals or depots, the number of patients are to be included here, the names being shown in A. F. A. 36.

_____ Signature of Commander.

_____ Date of Despatch.

Place _____ For information of the A.G.'s Office at the Base.

Officers and men who have become casuals, been transferred or joined since last report.

Date _____

Regtl. Number	Rank	Name	Corps	Nature of casualty, or name of unit from or to which transferred	Date of being struck off or coming on the ration return	Remarks*

* State whether absence is of a permanent or temporary nature, adding, in the case of casuals from wounds or disease, any available information for communication to the relatives.

Only additional information regarding "wanting to complete," and sufficient information to explain the difference between
the present and previous week's effective strength is to be entered on this side.

WAR DIARY
For 12th Bn Suffolk Regt

From 1/1/18
To 28/2/18

Originals
(Volume 21)

17
21

Demands made on this sheet should consist of personnel required from the Base only, and should not include any demands for personnel which can be completed by promotions or appointments within the unit.

Perforated Sheet giving detail of personnel and horses wanting to complete, shown on Army Form B. 213.

No. of Report _____

Detail of Wanting to Complete.	Drivers						Gunners	Smith Gunners	Range Takers	Farriers		Shoeing, or Shoeing and Carriage Smiths	Cold Shoers	Wheelers			Saddlers or Harness Makers	Blacksmiths	Bricklayers and Masons	Carpenters and Joiners	Fitters & Turners (R.E.)		Fitters		Wireless	Plumbers	Electricians		Signalmen	Engine Drivers		Air Line Men	Permanent Line Men	Operators, Telegraph	Cablemen	Brigade Section Pioneers	General-duty Pioneers	Signallers	Instrument Repairers	Motor Cyclist	Motor Cyclist Artificers	Telephonists	Clerks	Machine Gunners	Armament Artificers		Armourers	Storemen	Privates	W.O's. and N.C.O's. (by ranks) not included in trade columns					TOTAL to agree with wanting to complete		Horses				
	R.A.	R.E.	A.S.C.	Car	Lorry	Steam				Serjeants	Corporals			R.A.	H.T.	M.T.					Wood	Iron	R.A.				Ordinary	W.T.		Loco.	Field															Fitters	Range Finders									Officers	Other Ranks	Riding	Draught	Heavy Draught	Pack
CAVALRY																																																											
R.A.																																																											
R.E.																																																											
INFANTRY																																																											
R.A.M.C.																																																											
A.O.C.																																																											
A.V.C.																																																											

Remarks :—

_____ Signature of Commander.

_____ Unit.

_____ Formation to which attached.

_____ Date of Despatch.

(6305) Wt. W2927/M2226. 1,250,000. 6/17. McA. & W., Ltd. (E1348). Forms B2138/8.   [P.T.O.

Sheet I — WAR DIARY or INTELLIGENCE SUMMARY — 12th Bn Suffolk Regt.
Army Form C. 2118.

Place	Date	Hour	Summary of Events and Information	Remarks and references to Appendices
	February 1918			
BULLECOURT	1		In Front Line. Quiet. Relieved by 13th Bn YORKSHIRE REGT. & moved to Support outside ECOUST. AWC	
ECOUST	2		In Support. Quiet. AWC	
	3		In Support. 8 Aeroplane bombs dropped outside Bn HQ. at 8.30am. Quiet. AWC	
	4		In Support. AWC	
	5		In Support. A Draft of 10 Officers + 197 O.R. arrived from 9th Batt. AWC	
	6		In Support. AWC	
BULLECOURT	7		In Support. Relieved the 13th YORKS in Front Line. AWC	
	8		In Front Line. At 6.30am the enemy fired red lights along the whole Div front & about 6.35 put down a heavy barrage chiefly on the left Batt. Our casualties 4 OR slightly wounded. AWC	
	9		Our Artillery put a heavy pre-arranged barrage on enemy trenches from 5.40am to 6.15am drawing very little retaliation. Remainder of the day quiet. AWC	
	10		Quiet. AWC	
	11		Quiet. AWC	

WAR DIARY
or
INTELLIGENCE SUMMARY

Army Form C. 2118.

Place	Date	Hour	Summary of Events and Information	Remarks and references to Appendices
BOLLECOURT	13	10.50 am	fire a long burst at all able sun in enemy trenches during the afternoon. Relieved by 4/4 London number T.MOR & no5 in Relief to CLONMEL CAMP HAMELINCOURT ditto	
MORY	15		CLONMEL CAMP. HAMELINCOURT	
HAMELINCOURT	14			
"	15		"	
"	16		"	
"	17		"	
"	18		Working parties on defense lines in night. 550 o.r.	
"	19		" 550 o.r.	
"	20		" 550 o.r.	
"	21		"	
"	22		"	
"	23		"	
"	24		"	
"	25		"	

Sheet III — WAR DIARY — 12th Bn Suffolk Regt.

Place	Date	Hour	Summary of Events and Information	Remarks and references to Appendices
	Febry			
HAMELINCOURT	26		CLONMEL CAMP. HAMELINCOURT. Working party on defence line at night. 550 O.R.	AAI
"	27		" " " .	AAI
BAILLEULMONT	28		Marched to Billets at BAILLEULMONT.	AAI

A.A. Snow
Capt for Lt Col.
Cmdg. 12th Bn Suffolk Regt.

12th 13th Assam Regt.

	A.R.	
17	35	750
49		913
17		303
		10

Return
of for List
by N.B. Lutterworth

Strength of Bn. Bn. Jul. 1st
Strength of 13. Bn. Jul. 31.
Reinforcements during month
Casualties in Action "
Lost at sea

Officers - Regiment dinner on 12th

Major L. Pirie   Jones facing 2.10
"   F. R. Bacon   "   "   2.10
"   A. Johnson   "   "   2.10
"   E. J. Taylor   "   "   2.10
"   A. J. Neill   "   "   2.10

Captain R. Boylan M.C.
"   C. Robertson Johnson
Lieutenant A. B. Boylan   Champion   9th B. Major
Major E. Hopkirk   Champion facing   gun " King
"   A. Home   " "   "
Lt J. N. Manley   " "   "
" B. L. Jones   12th
" C. E. Lewis
" H. Harrison
" J. Harris
" F. Clark
" W. G. Parks

Aldwin
Capt. Hilton
for 12th Bn Officers Regt.

40th Division.
121st Infantry Brigade.

WAR DIARY

12th BATTALION

THE SUFFOLK REGIMENT

MARCH 1.9.1.8

Attached :- Report on Operations 21st-26th

WAR DIARY or INTELLIGENCE SUMMARY.
Sheet 1 12th Bn Suffolk Regt 121/40 Army Form C. 2118.
(Erase heading not required.)

Vol 2

Place	Date	Hour	Summary of Events and Information	Remarks and references to Appendices
MAP LENS. 11	March 1918			
BAILLEULMONT	1-12		In billets. Training. On 13th marched to Camp at BLAIRVILLE	AH6
BLAIRVILLE	13-20		In Camp Training	AH6
In action corps	21-22			
army lines	23-24		In action continuously	AH
	25			
BIENVILLERS	26th		Battn withdrawn from action	AH
SUS-ST-LEGER	27th		Marching to SUS-ST-LEGER	AH
" " "	28th		In billets.	AH
" " "	29th		Marched to BAILLEUL-AUX-CORNAILLES to billets	AH
BAILLEUL-AUX-CORNAILLES	30th		Battalion proceeded by buses to billets close to NEUF BEQUIN (Map Hazebrouck 1/100,000)	AH
NEUF BEQUIN	31st		In billets	AH

R.H. Sims
Capt & adjt
for Major
Coy 12th Bn Suffolk Regt.

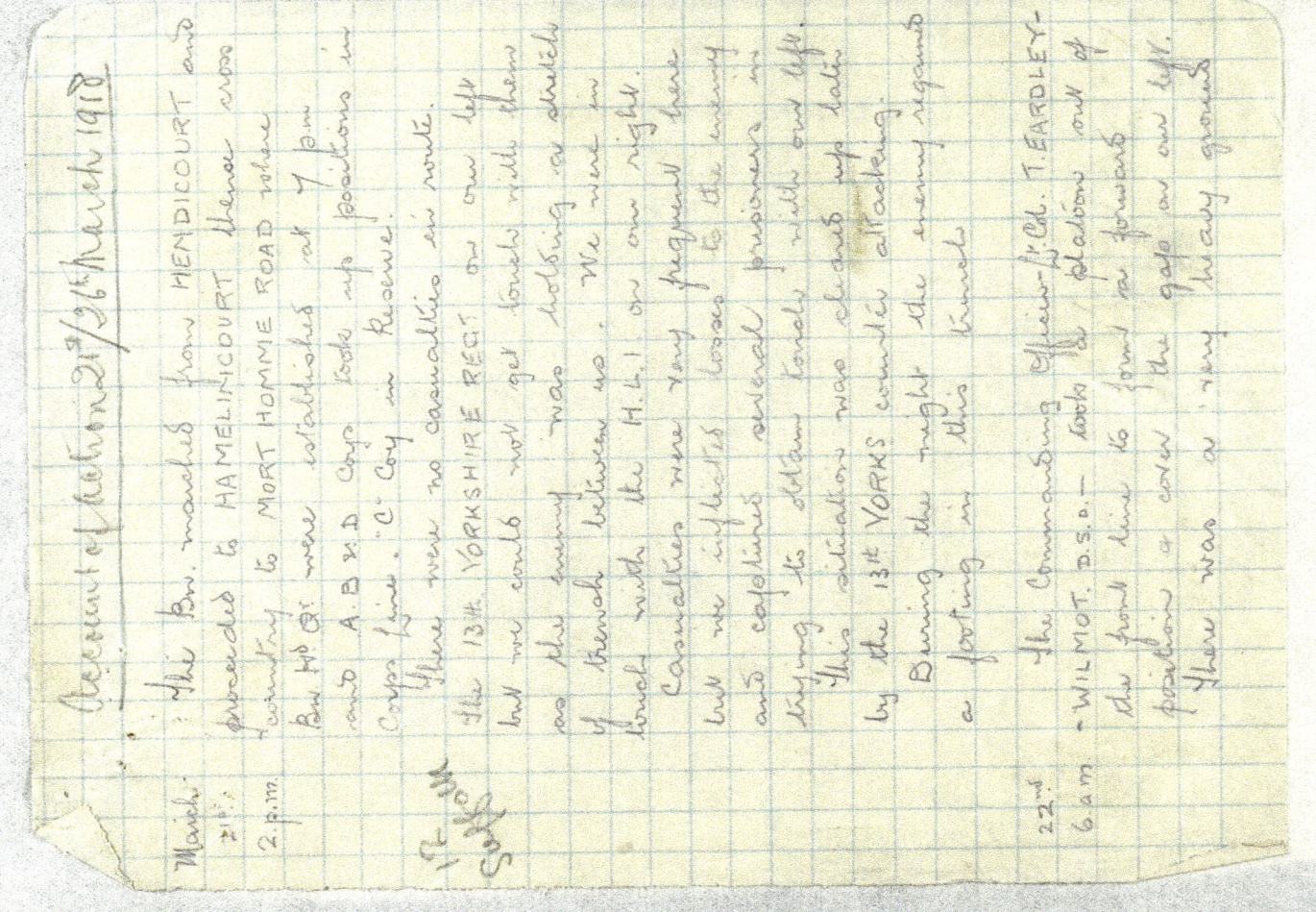

Account of Action 21st/26th March 1918

March 21st 2 p.m.
The Bn. marched from HENDICOURT and proceeded to HAMELINCOURT thence cross country to MORT HOMME ROAD where Bn. HQrs. were established at 7 p.m. and A. B. & D. Coys took up positions in Coppice – "C" Coy in Reserve.
There were no casualties en route.

1st from Suffolk
The 13th YORKSHIRE REGT. on our left but we could not get touch with them as the enemy was holding a switch of trench between us. We were in touch with the H.L.I. on our right.
Casualties were very frequent here but we inflicted losses to the enemy and captured several prisoners in trying to obtain touch with our left.
The situation was cleared up later by the 13th YORKS counter attacking.
During the night the enemy regained a footing in this knuckle

22nd 6 a.m.
The Commanding Officer Lt. Col. T. EARDLEY-WILMOT. D.S.O. took his station on of the front line to find a forward position and later the gap on our left. There was a very heavy ground

2./

knew' and the enemy snipers had taken up good positions, and sniped the C.O. and the artillery liason officer who was with him, killing them both. There were also several casualties amongst the men.

The A/Spitalier - Capt A. M. CROSS m.c. + the Adjutant - Capt D. M. CROSS m.c. met them took command.

We continued to suffer casualties from enemy M.Gs and also our own Artillery.

22.? The enemy attacked considerably to
2.p.m. our left but we could get no definite information as to the situation and
4.p.m. later found he was massing on our own front. We opened L.G. + rifle fire upon him and got good results from the Artillery. His casualties were heavy here

5.p.m. The LG fire was weakening and we were under heavy enemy M.G. fire and at 5.p.m. received information to the effect that enemy was attacking with on our right. Later we saw them

6:30 p.m. advancing and driving our troops back.

3

March 22nd 6 p.m.

A heavy enemy artillery barrage was put down on the MORT HOMME ROAD and a little later we were attacked in force. We sent up the S.O.S. signal and this came off, and our artillery put down a good barrage. By then we knew both our flanks were "in the air" the enemy having the trench on our right & left, and our forward Coys were ordered to fall back on the Army Line. The barrage was obtained, but we afraid in arrived too late as no officer or O.R. of either of the 3 Coys returned. Meanwhile B. Hd Qr + C Coy retired to the Army Line. B.N.Qr established in MORY COPSE. Patrols sent out, and suffered casualties.

about 9 p.m.

the Second-in-Command arrived and took over, but had previously seen the enemy on MORY–ECOUST ROAD 200x above L'ABBAYE and formed a block at Road junction there of A. & S.H. and others under an officer. Two Corps Reserve Btt: - 20th Middlesex were sent for and a line formed from Army line in front MORY COPSE 16

about 9.10 p.m.

SUNKEN ROAD behind MORY COPSE thence

March 22ⁿᵈ 1.

about 9.10 p.m. along SUNKEN ROAD to cross roads MORY we got touch with 2/6th LEICESTERS. The Army Line was held by the enemy on both our flanks we had a M.G. Section on our left.

11 p.m. to 1 a.m. The enemy attacked but we held him on our front. We pushed round on our right through MORY & up the Sunken Road also round MORY COPSE and up Sunken Road which was on the Left. Orders were come to move back Vickers Sunken Road and under very heavy M.G. + rifle fire from the front and both flanks then more rifles accomplished and a trench running at right angles to the Sunken Road occupied, and the Vickers then faced both flanks. The M.G. Section also took up position in this trench.

23ʳᵈ
1 - 4 a.m. All touch has again been lost with other units and as the enemy fire died down the troops were moved in column of route - under cover of darkness - across country

2/6 dieselen.
Then was no nice Galloeen
2/4 dieselen (or so einigy)
linens to meaur. dew?

5/

March 23rd
1 - 4 a.m. towards ERVILLERS then left to ERVILLERS-MORY ROAD, extended and advanced towards MORY with right on road. Touch was again obtained with 2/6th LEICESTERS who had extended with left on road.

5-6 a.m. Raising grounds was selected and the men dug in under enemy M.G. fire no touch with our left and enemy occupying crest immediately in front of us and WEST of MORY.

6 a.m. - 8 p.m. Continuous M.G. fire and H.V. and heavy shrapnel on our position all day suffered considerable casualties. Youens obtained touch with left during afternoon. Patrols out all night. Enemy evacuated crest in front of us.

11. p.m. E.A. bombs our position dropping 7 bombs, no casualties.

March 24th
5 a.m.- 8 p.m. Night 23rd 24th comparatively quiet but enemy shells our position and sprays us with M.G's all day. opposite + roads registered with H.V. + heavy shrapnel. Several casualties.

6

March 24th
10.30 p.m.   S.O.S. sent up on our left flank and very heavy Artillery and M.G. barrage opens by both sides. Enemy attacks on wide front on our left — MORY 16 ERVILLERS — and drove troops on our left through our position. We faced left & ones opens L.G. + Rifle fire & held up the advance for some considerable time. He was too strong for us however & we retired on MORY ERVILLERS ROAD and again held him up. Our casualties were very heavy and the enemy in greatly superior numbers, and under heavy fire we took up a position in front of the ERVILLERS-BEHAGNIES ROAD, which we held during the remainder of the night.

March 25th
5. a.m.
12. NOON.   Enemy clearly seen digging M.G. positions and the snipers did good execution. Movement of many casualties all the morning.

3. p.m.   Enemy attacks in force on wide front but did not reach our trench. He passed through on

March 25th.
3 p.m. our night and the 4/5th
Guards retired leaving our left
flank open.

The troops occupying the
position taken up above
consists of men from 12th Suffolks
20th Middlesex, 21st Middlesex + about
200 men who has been reorganised
and distributed in this system
amongst 7/o Leicesters, 10th and 11th Essex
Yorkshires.

8 p.m. At 8 p.m. thin line was
evacuated and the remands of
the Bn. marched to AYETTE where
they spent the remainder of the
night.

March 26th
8 a.m. Battalion marches to BIENVILLERS
and took up an outpost position.
11.45 p.m. Battalion marches on HABARCQ
and at 6 a.m. halts then marches

March 27th to SUS St LEGER.
6 a.m. 22 Regimental Officers and the
M.O. went into the fight
and only the M.O. and 1
Regimental Officer returned to
duty. All others all [killed?]

	Officers	Other Ranks
STRENGTH FOR 2nd MARCH, 1918.	50	1003
STRENGTH FOR 29th MARCH, 1918.	26	644
CASUALTIES DURING MONTH.	21	346
REINFORCEMENTS DURING MONTH.	-	19

CASUALTIES DURING MONTH - OFFICERS :-

Lieut Col. T. Eardley-Wilmot. D.S.O.	Killed and Missing.
2/Lieutenant L. Scott.	" " "
Lieutenant J. E. Hamblin.	" " "
2/Lieutenant G. R. Pedrick.	Killed.
2/Lieutenant E. L. Turner.	Wounded and Missing.
2/Lieutenant A. W. Barnard.	" " "
Captain R. England. M.C.	Missing.
Lieutenant H. C. Mathew. M.C.	"
Lieutenant G. Hopkins.	"
2/Lieutenant A. J. Wells.	"
2/Lieutenant J. A. Blanch.	"
2/Lieutenant S. E. Clark.	"
2/Lieutenant G. Hallsmith. D.S.O.	"
2/Lieutenant G. T. Taylor.	"
2/Lieutenant C. H. Hitchcock.	"
Captain A. M. Cross. M.C.	Wounded.
2/Lieutenant G. F. Franklin.	"
2/Lieutenant R. Tricker.	"
2/Lieutenant R. E. Gooch.	"
2/Lieutenant L. H. Knowles. M.C.	"
2/Lieutenant C. H. Cockerton.	"

40th Division.
121st Infantry Brigade.

WAR DIARY

12th BATTALION

THE SUFFOLK REGIMENT.

APRIL 1918

Narrative of Operations 9th-13th April.

April 1918 **WAR DIARY or INTELLIGENCE SUMMARY** **12th Battn Suffolk Regt** Army Form C. 2118.

Sheet I.

Place	Date	Hour	Summary of Events and Information	Remarks and references to Appendices
BOIS GRENIER SECTOR	1st/2nd		Relieved 2/8th King Liverpool Regt in front line. Nil.	
"	2nd/3rd		In front line. Nil.	
"	4th/5th		In support in billets in FLEURBAIX. Nil.	
FLEURBAIX	6th/7th/8th		" " " " " " Nil.	
"	9th/10th/11th/12th		Enemy attacked 11 mile front. Battalion in action at 9.30 am continued in action until 4.30 pm 13th April. Nil.	Narrative of operations attached
BAVINCHOVE	13th		Marched to BAVINCHOVE & bivouacked. Nil.	
ST OMER	14th		Marched to billets at ST MARTIN AU LAERT near ST OMER. Nil.	
"	15-20th		In billets refitting & training at " " " Nil.	
BAVINCHOVE	21st		Marched to tents at BAVINCHOVE. Nil.	
HERZEELE	22nd		" " " at HERZEELE. Nil.	
"	23rd		In tents at HERZEELE. Nil.	
RWELD	24th		Marched to tents at RWELD. Nil.	
"	25th/26th/27th		Work on Defence line in RWELD area. Nil.	
PROVEN	28th		Marched to tents in PROVEN area. Nil.	
"	29th		Work on POPERINGHE line. Nil.	

WAR DIARY or INTELLIGENCE SUMMARY

Army Form C. 2118.

12th Batta. Suffolk Regt.

April 1918

Sheet II

Place	Date	Hour	Summary of Events and Information	Remarks and references to Appendices
ROVEN	30		Training. etc.	

Arthur Cpl 6/5/01
12th Suffolk Regt

NARRATIVE OF OPERATIONS OF 12TH SUFFOLKS
FROM 9th/13th APRIL, 1918.

9th
4.15 a.m. A very heavy bombardment by enemy was put down on front line and FLEURBAIX defences, a tremendous amount of gas being used.
The Battalion 'stood to' and at 7 a.m. the defences were manned as follows:-

7 a.m.
"A" Coy. "A" Coy. in reserve round DURHAM POST.
"B" Coy. Manned the 7 posts of the defences, i.e. from ABEL Post on right to LIMIT Post on left.
"C" Coy. MANN. In posts round MOULIN FARM.
"D" Coy. Manned trenches South of CANTEEN FARM.

10 a.m. Orders received from Bde. H.Q. to move "C" Coy. forward, join up LIMIT Post and CANTEEN FARM.
"A" Coy. reinforced "B" Coy. Patrol sent forward towards CROIX BLANCHE was fired upon from the Cross Roads.
Enemy party estimated at about 60. Patrol fired upon the enemy who then moved in an EASTERLY direction.

10.30 a.m. Battalion H.Q. moved from FLEURBAIX to PORT à CLOUS and party of 50 Hd.Qr. personnel moved forward to trenches forward of RUE DELPIERRE and later reinforced "C" Coy. WEST of LIMIT Post. About this time message received from CROIX BLANCHE patrol reporting large party of enemy cyclists moving EAST along the RUE des LOMBARDS.

11 a.m. The whole line now came under heavy machine gun fire from the enemy who had established himself in the "Subsidiary Line". Our L.Gs. were occupying positions in concrete emplacements and in shell holes in front of our Line.
3 L.Gs. were put out of action by enemy fire, and 1 gun being blown up by a shell and the team killed.
The fighting was severe and continuous, and very heavy losses inflicted on the enemy, who continued to move in sections in single file across our front towards the WEST.

4.30 p.m. Both flanks in the air, and after consultation it was decided to fight a rearguard action, and under covering fire of L.Gs. the garrison moved back and filled a gap between the 16th Royal Scots on right and the 11th Suffolks on left. Here they dug in and held on all night. Our casualties were very heavy, particularly "B" and "C" Coys.
Bn. Hd.Qrs. had been cut off from remainder of Battalion and came under enemy M.G. fire from RUE DE BIACHE and enemy was reported moving EAST long MAIN ROAD and Railway from BAS ST MAUR.
Headquarters moved to LEVEL CROSSING H.14.a.7.4 and later to FORT·ROMPU where about 60 stragglers were collected and the Road Junction and Village held. My main position was in an orchard at H.8.c.5.3. The enemy formed up three times and attacked FORT ROMPU from about H.13.b.central, but he was held up by our fire. He had M.Gs. on the road at about H.7.d.7b.2b. The enemy continued to dribble along the railway towards RUE DORMOIRE. I had previously got touch with the 16th Royal Scots Regt. and they were taking up a position from Cross Roads H.8.b.4.1 to H.1b.b.b0.00

6.30 p.m. Word received 16th Royal Scots were in position and in trenches with "B" Coy. 12th Suffolks on left, and Headquarters moved back taking stragglers, and took up position from X Roads H.8.b.4.1. to River LYS at about H.7.b.8.9. The line now ran from H.7.b.8.9 to H.8.b.4.1 held by part of 12th Bn. Suffolk Regt., Headquarters and stragglers, thence to H.1b.d.7.5 by 16th Royal Scots to

This rearguard action mentioned in "Times" 16th April

2.

6.30 p.m.	H.22.a.1.1. East along grid to H.16.c.80.00 N.E. H.16.d.2.8 by "B" & "C" Coys. Suffolks,- where we were in touch with 11th Suffolks, who had absorbed "D" Coy. 12th Suffolks. "A" Coy. in support to "B" & "C" Coys. in H.16.c. Headquarters, consisting 2 Officers & 7 runners, amalgamated with 16th Royal Scots at ERQUINGHEM and came under orders of 101st Brigade.
10th.	
8 a.m.	Heavy shelling and M.G. fire on our front and left followed by enemy attack. Our troops gradually driven back towards ERQUINGHEM. Fighting continued throughout the day and at 4 p.m. orders received to cross River LYS and hold ERQUINGHEM SWITCH from LANCASHIRE POST to WIGAN POST. This was done in conjunction with 16th Royal Scots, but the enemy had crossed to the north of the River LYS early in the afternoon at BAC ST MAUR and was gradually working N.E. We were in touch with 102nd Brigade on our left but the right was kpen.
11th.	
2 a.m.	Orders received to make our way towards NIEPPE and hold Railway, where we came under orders of 102nd Bde. We had joined up with the 13th Yorks Regt. and details of 20th Middlesex Regt. and Lt.Col. C.E.M. Richards, M.C. 20th Bn. Middlesex Regt. took command of the 3 units, 121st-Brigade.
8 a.m.	Ordered to take a position in B.8.c.d. and dug in roughly from B.8.c.20.80 to MILL B.8.d.4.5.
2 p.m.	Reports received that enemy had broken front line and was holding LA RUE DU SAC and the Battalion was ordered to counter attack and restore the position. Formed up for the attack in H.8.b. with left on road at 80.00 and right about B.9.a.2.3. in following order :- "C" Coy. 2 L.Gs. first wave "A" & "B" 2 L.Gs. second wave, a few of "D" Coy. and some Australian-R.Es. in reserve. The attacking lines moved off and took the buildings at PAPOT B.3.c., killing a number of the enemy and taking 1 prisoner. The enemy retired in a Northerly direction but left several M.Gs. and a large number of snipers in buildings in LA RUE DU SAC. The Second line reinforced the first line and L.G. positions takene up.
5 p.m.	orders were received not to press the attack but to hold on to our position until 8.30 p.m. Our casualties were heavy - about 70.- in this attack, but we inflicted heavy casualties on the enemy.
8.30 p.m.	At 8.30 p.m. moved back in open order, the forward line passing through the support line then covering the support as they moved back on to a line held by the Monmouth Regt.
9.0 p.m.	Marched to LA CRECHE, arriving about 11 p.m. and lined a road, as reserve, and at 4.30 a.m. marched to STRAZEELE,
12th 4.30 a.m.	arriving about 8 9 a.m., where we dug in, and were again reserve. The night was quiet and we were not in action, but our position was shelled and a forward L.G. post knocked out.
13th. 4.30 p.m.	Marched to HONDEGHEM ROAD arriving about 7.30 p.m. Here we joined our transport and at 9.15 p.m. marched to BAVINCHOVE, arriving about 11.30 p.m. and bivouaced for the night.
14th. 9.15 a.m.	Marched to ST. OMER to Billets.

APRIL 17th. 1918.

Lieut.Colonel,
Commanding 12th Bn. Suffolk Regiment.

	Officers	Other Ranks
STRENGTH FOR 27th April, 1918.	36	803.
STRENGTH FOR 1st June, 1918.	11	51.
CASUALTIES DURING MONTH.	N I L.	
REINFORCEMENTS DURING MONTH.	N I L.	

AWARDS DURING MONTH :-

London Gazette dated 28th May, 1918.

T/Lieut.Col. L. Lloyd, D.S.O.   Awarded Bar to D.S.O.
T/Captain A.A. Smee, M.C.   MENTION.
T/Lieut: M.P. Richards, M.C.   MENTION.
T/2/Lieut. G. M.Lismith, D.S.O.   MENTION.

T/Lieut.Col. L. Lloyd, D.S.O. Awarded Bar to D.S.O.
(Divisional Routine Orders dated 29/5/18.)

T/Captain A.A. Smee. Awarded Military Cross.
(Divisional Routine Orders dated 28/5/18.)

Captain F.O.H. Gass. R.A.M.C. (S.R.) attached 12th Suffolks.
Awarded Military Cross.
(Divisional Routine Orders dated 15/5/18.)

3/10300 Sergeant Smith, A.C. Awarded D.C.M.
(Divisional Routine Orders dated 28/5/18.)

50012 Private Hearns M. Awarded D.C.M.
(Divisional Routine Orders dated 15/5/18.)

9565 L/Corpl. Broome, E.C. Awarded Military Medal.
(Divisional Routine Orders dated 18/5/18.)

	Officers	Other Ranks
STRENGTH FOR 30th MARCH, 1918.	26	644
STRENGTH FOR 27th April, 1918.	36	803
CASUALTIES DURING MONTH.	6	417
REINFORCEMENTS DURING MONTH.	17	621

CASUALTIES DURING MONTH - OFFICERS :-

2/Lieutenant C.F. SMITH. (Att.T.M.B.)   Killed.
Captain   H.A. REDDING. M.C.   Wounded.
2/Lieutenant E.A. WILLIAMS. M.C.   "
2/Lieutenant H.A. PANTON.   "
2/Lieutenant A. JOHNSON.   "
2/Lieutenant S.H. HABERSHON.   Missing.

REINFORCEMENTS DURING MONTH - OFFICERS :-

2/Lieutenant G.F. FRANKLIN.   Returned from Hos. Wounded.
Major   A.M. CROSS. M.C.   "   "   "   "
Lieutenant   G.A.B. GILBERT.   Joined for Duty.
2/Lieutenant C.E. KELLY.   "   "   "
Captain   A.H. GUINNESS.   "   "   "
Captain   A.R.R. COX.   "   "   "
2/Lieutenant B.V.P. KENDALL.   "   "   "
Lieutenant   H.O. ASHTON.   "   "   "
2/Lieutenant G.R. POCKLINGTON.   "   "   "
Lieutenant   F. JAGGARD.   "   "   "
2/Lieutenant R.H. ATTWELL.   "   "   "
2/Lieutenant R.W. AYLIFFE.   "   "   "
2/Lieutenant C.T. GOOKIE.   "   "   "
2/Lieutenant G.F. THEEDOM. D.C.M.   "   "   "
2/Lieutenant A.J. WRIGHT.   "   "   "
Captain   S.W. CHURCH.   "   "   "
2/Lieutenant T. MACE.   "   "   "

May 1918 WAR DIARY or INTELLIGENCE SUMMARY 12th Bn Suffolk Regt. Army Form C. 2118.

Vol 24

Place	Date	Hour	Summary of Events and Information	Remarks and references to Appendices
	MAY			
PROVEN	1st		In camp. AAS.	
TERDEGHEM	2nd		Marched to camp at TERDEGHEM. AAS	
KLINDERBELK	3rd		Marched to camp at KLINDERBELK N.E. ST. OMER. AAS	
"	3.4.5.6		In camp at KLINDERBELK. On 5th May Battalion reduced to Training Cadre establishment. 21 Officers 670 other ranks despatched to Base Depot for reposting. AAS	
"	6th		In camp. Preparing census of accommodation in given area & preparing large scale map. AAS	
"	7th-17th		In camp " " " " " " " AAS	
SERCUS	18th		Marched to camp at SERCUS. AAS	
"	19th-29th		In camp. Siting Defence lines etc. AAS	
NORDPEENE	30th		By lorries to camp at NORDPEENE. AAS	
"	31st		In camp. AAS	

A.A. Snow
Capt & adj
for Lt Col Commanding
12th (S) Bn The Suffolk Regt.